START & RUN A
PERSONAL
HISTORY
BUSINESS

START & RUN A
PERSONAL
HISTORY
BUSINESS

Jennifer Campbell

Self-Counsel Press
(a division of)
International Self-Counsel Press Ltd.
USA   Canada

Self-Counsel Press acknowledges the financial support of the Government of Canada through the Canada Book Fund (CBF) for our publishing activities.

Printed in Canada.

First edition: 2011; Reprinted: 2012

Library and Archives Canada Cataloguing in Publication

Campbell, Jennifer, 1953–
    Start & run a personal history business / Jennifer Campbell.

    ISBN 978-1-77040-058-0

    1. Historiography. 2. Biography — Authorship. 3. New business enterprises — Management.
I. Title.
CT22.C36 2010   906   C2010-902050-2

Cover and inside images
Copyright©iStockphoto/Fading memories/Anyka

Self-Counsel Press
(a division of)
International Self-Counsel Press Ltd.

Bellingham, WA   North Vancouver, BC
USA   Canada

CONTENTS

For Jamie and David

ACKNOWLEDGMENTS

I couldn't have written this book without the help of the following people: first and foremost Bill, for his endless patience and support; my generous, talented colleagues at the Association of Personal Historians; Barry Baines, Dan Curtis, Linda Coffin, Linda Blachman, and Kurt Medina for their contributions to this book; Eileen Velthuis and Richard Day of Self-Counsel Press, who saw the potential of this project and shepherded it through; and the storytellers who trust me to help them tell their life stories. Each of them inspires me and touches my heart, and I'm grateful to them for enriching my own life story.

— Jennifer Campbell

NOTICE TO READERS

1
THE WORLD OF PERSONAL HISTORY

1. What Is a Personal Historian? An Introduction

When I tell people I'm a personal historian, sometimes I hear, "A what?" or, "Like, you do genealogy?" After a quick explanation — "Well, genealogy and personal history are related fields," — I explain that I help people tell their life stories and publish them in heirloom books for their families and future generations. Within a minute, they're telling me about a relative who's led such an interesting life who really should do his memoirs. Or, sadly, about a relative who just passed away and used to tell great stories but no one got a chance to write them down, and now that branch of the family has lost its history. It seems everyone knows somebody who needs a personal historian.

What does a personal historian do? A personal historian steps into other people's lives for a brief, intense time, asking questions about their background, ancestors, events, and experiences that shaped their lives, relationships, foibles, struggles, accomplishments, regrets, highlights, and low lights — whatever memories, thoughts, feelings, and reflections they wish to talk about and have preserved. In a typical book project, a personal historian guides a person through the telling of his or her life's stories (or some aspect of his or her life) for a number of hours, records the interviews, transcribes word-for-word, and organizes, edits, and rewrites the transcripts into a polished narrative. Once the manuscript is completed, photos and memorabilia can be added to enhance the story, and everything is laid out in book form and published for the author, his or her family, and friends.

In *Start & Run a Personal History Business*, space dictates that I focus only on personal history books, but these "how-to" guidelines and practices can be applied to a wide variety of products and formats, from audio or video recordings, books, quilts and art collages, to multimedia presentations on DVD. See Chapter 15 about some of the exciting possible ways to capture and preserve memories.

Personal historians preserve not only life stories, but also the histories of businesses, towns, families, places of worship, organizations, special-interest groups and ethnic groups, or groups such as veterans or hospice patients. Not everyone calls themselves a personal historian: there's the corporate (or business) historian, community historian, public historian, legacy writer, biographer, memoir writer, ghostwriter, and oral historian, to name a few. A videobiographer is another professional in the field, using a camera and sophisticated equipment and software. Editors and coaches work on memoirs that are already written or are being written. Workshop leaders teach memoir writing. Others specialize in photograph restoration, archiving, writing obituaries, delivering eulogies (as "funeral celebrants"), graphic design, printing, and binding.

What these professions have in common is a passion for preserving the past. I hope that *Start & Run a Personal History Business* ignites that passion in you, too.

2. The World of Personal History

2.1 A business that's timely — and timeless

This is a "hot" profession: a young industry with vast potential for income and growth.

When I started Heritage Memoirs in 2002, I just wanted a creative outlet for my interviewing, writing, and editing skills. Through my father's death and my mother's dementia, I had lost my own family stories and thought there could possibly be a business helping other people avoid that loss. I never dreamed that, five years later, the *Financial Post* would name what I was doing one of the top ten business opportunities, to "serve the needs of luxury-seeking, time-pressed and suddenly health-conscious Canadians." It said: "Personal Memoirs. Create a record of peoples' parents or ancestors as a memorialist and put it in a handsome bound book. Must be able to write."

Interest in the field has caught on like wildfire. Personal historians and their clients have been featured in hundreds of major news outlets such as *The Wall Street Journal*, *The New York Times*, *The Toronto Star*, *AARP: The Magazine*, *The Philadelphia Inquirer*, *Money*, *Worth*, *Real Simple*, *O Magazine* and on television programs like *The Oprah Show*. It's no surprise the media loves stories about personal history projects. They have all the elements of a feel-good feature article: human interest, history, connecting generations, celebrating the "ordinary" person, family values. And there is the unique nature of the product itself: beautiful, one-of-a-kind books that will last for generations. It's history — living history — in the making!

With a growing fascination in memoirs and genealogy, it was only a matter of time before entrepreneurs saw an opportunity to help people with their projects, but the term "personal historian" didn't come into the mainstream until after 1995 when an enterprising group met in an eighteenth-century inn in New England. Mainly writers, they had carved out a niche market, getting paid to help people tell their life stories, and wanted a supportive network to discuss advances in the field, interviewing and recording techniques, resources, pricing, and to otherwise build a business doing what they were doing. But what should they call themselves? They tossed around the phrases "memoir writer," "historian," "biography writer," and others, and finally settled on personal historian. It did the best job of capturing what we do: help tell and preserve the history of a person. That group formed the Association of Personal Historians (APH), and it remains the premier group for "entrepreneur story-savers."

2.2 The memoirs and genealogy phenomenon: Capturing the moment — Past, present, and future

In the past 15 years, interest in memoirs, genealogy, and family history has exploded. Memoirs consistently dominate the bestseller lists, and not just those written by celebrities (or their ghostwriters). People are reading memoirs of everyday people, like Frank McCourt with his Pulitzer-prize winning memoir, *Angela's Ashes*. No longer are memoirs only written by the elderly. The midlife memoir is quite common and, as I was writing this book, two *American Idol* contestants, barely out of their teens, were reported to be writing their memoirs. Like peeking into someone's diary, we are fascinated with other people's lives; the appeal of the memoir crosses all economic, geographic, racial, ethnic, and age segments.

Along with reading about other people's lives comes the passionate pursuit of writing about our own. Historically, writing one's reminiscences was reserved for the elite; stories of everyday people, especially marginalized factions like the poor or women, were largely lost. Today there is a groundswell of memoir writers, meeting in libraries, church basements, and online to support each other as they document their experiences and pass them down to future generations. Thousands of websites are also devoted to the memoir genre.

Genealogy — tracing your family history through your ancestors — is said to be the most popular pastime in North America and many other parts of the world. Largely thanks to the Internet, enthusiasts are almost obsessively researching their roots and discovering their lineage. At the time of writing this book, the Ancestry.com and Ancestry.ca websites have more than one million members and hundreds of thousands of forums. Television programs like *Ancestors in the Attic* and *Who Do You Think You Are?* attract millions of viewers. And following close on the heels of genealogy is the incredibly popular hobby of scrapbooking. All these trends — memoirs, genealogy, and scrapbooking — are about capturing "momentous memories": the moments and times of our lives that are meant to be shared with those close to us, now and in the future.

But what's behind this phenomenon?

2.3 Honoring the past in a rapidly changing world

With technology changing our world so rapidly, we are realizing the need to capture the "old ways" — before everyone forgets what they were like. We're honoring the past like never before, and are hungry for firsthand accounts of people who were there and who themselves are living history. Before they pass away and their stories are lost forever, we are interviewing and recording Holocaust survivors, war veterans, refugees, workers whose jobs are disappearing, and others. Their stories are being preserved in hundreds of institutions, museums, and archives and produced in documentaries, movies, television programs, and books.

The stories behind heritage buildings and objects are gaining respect, too. If you watch *Antiques Roadshow*, you've probably noticed how the value skyrockets when the item has a story behind it. Buyers are willing to pay handsomely for "provenance," which refers to an object's origin, because it gives the item authenticity and a place in history. Auctioneers have known and capitalized on this for years.

It's happening in the business world, too, as more and more corporations honor their history, appeal to nostalgia, and leverage their stories. Grainy black and white photos of the first hamburger stand or gas station abound in advertisements. Some personal historians specialize in corporate history books, which because of their scope and high quality can easily run upward of $40,000 and well beyond — a lucrative niche market.

Part of the reason we are getting better at documenting our history is because it's easier to do so, thanks to the Internet; digital cameras and recorders; and computers and software programs. It's ironic that advancements in technology are fostering this passion for preserving the past.

2.4 The need for story

It's getting easier and faster to tell each other what's happening in our lives through email, Twitter, Facebook, text messaging, blogging, camera phones, etc., but many feel the "soul" has gone out of our communication. Most of it is brief, fleeting, cut-to-the-chase, and lacks the contemplation and careful composition that handwritten letters have. And much of it is lost forever in cyberspace. We're storing thousands of digital photos on our computers and CDs or DVDs, but what happens when the computer crashes or a particular piece of equipment becomes obsolete? The moments are being captured, but will they be preserved for the future? Will they be remembered? And what about the stories behind the photos?

People are craving meaningful connections — to ourselves, to each other, and to our roots and our future — and personal stories are a big part of that.

2.4a Once upon a (life) time: The power and endurance of story

Why is a life story a priceless gift for families, and for the storyteller? The world of personal histories is all about story, so let's start with one:

> One day, an anthropologist who was staying with and studying a primitive African tribe wanted to see what effect a television would have on the society, so he brought one into the village and hooked it up. People gathered around the TV day and night, staring in wonder. But after a few days, they drifted away and took up their regular daily routines again and largely ignored the talking box.
>
> The anthropologist was puzzled.
>
> "Aren't you interested in the TV?" he asked.
>
> A tribesman said, "Yes, it's very nice, but you see, we have our own storyteller."
>
> "Yes," said the anthropologist, "but the TV knows many more stories than your storyteller."
>
> "That may be true," said the tribesman, "but our storyteller knows *us*."

Though the term "personal history" may be relatively new, it is really an extension of an ancient tradition of telling — and listening to — stories of our "tribes": those closest to us. Those are the stories that resonate the loudest because they tell us where we've come from and help us understand ourselves. They provide context, connection, and continuity in a world that is increasingly busy and disconnected.

Storytelling is in our souls. For thousands of years, the elders of a family or society have used stories to teach, entertain, pass along wisdom, explain the world, share joy and heartache, and to preserve the history of the society, which was sometimes necessary for survival. Cave dwellers carved pictures of the hunt, and Egyptians saved recipes with hieroglyphics. Graffiti is the modern-day equivalent of "Kilroy was here." As cavemen, we used to share stories sitting around the fire. More recently, we'd sit around the supper table, and not that long ago, it was common to have three generations living together. Our society is in danger of losing the passing along of wisdom and experiences from generations. As well, because of the distractions of computers, TVs, and video games, we're a much more mobile and fractured society. People move away, parents divorce, and grandparents may not have the opportunity to verbally pass along family traditions, wisdom, and experience.

2.4b The magical bond created by storyteller and listener

No one will deny the immeasurable satisfaction of writing your memoirs, but it can be a daunting task, and not everyone has the skill, time, or physical and mental ability. Most people want to document their lives somehow but never get around to it, simply because it is so overwhelming. A personal historian can ensure everyone has the opportunity to save their stories, because almost everyone can talk. Telling, as opposed to writing, is a natural, easy-flowing way to express oneself; it's faster; and the storyteller doesn't have to worry about grammar, punctuation, paragraph breaks, and all those writerly concerns, as the storyteller can just talk as the personal historian records what he or she says and can write it down later.

Most important, there is an interested audience. One-on-one, the narrator talks about his or her life while the personal historian assumes the most important of tasks: listening. As the listener — the keeper of the stories — you hold a position of great honor and trust. Your client is counting on you to understand and interpret his or her stories, some of which he or she may never have breathed a word about before sitting down with you. This creates a real bond between you and the narrator. At the best of times, it's nothing less than a spiritual experience, as you share the drama, depth, and humanity of the moments. Emotions often run high, on both sides.

This special relationship is among the many rewards of being a personal historian. Most of your clients will agree that it's far more appealing than sitting alone at a computer staring at a blank screen.

2.5 Mind, body, and spirit

2.5a The baby boomers and memoirs

It's no accident that the surge of interest in journaling, memoirs, and family history has accompanied a more holistic approach to life. The Western world is discovering what has long been a tenet of Eastern philosophies and practice: There are undeniable connections between the mind, body, and spirit, and that we need health in all three areas in order to be happy and fulfilled. Baby boomers, generally, are more into healthy living, self-exploration, and self-discovery than any previous generation, and there are few activities more likely to enlighten than examining and documenting your own life. Baby boomers are not known as the "me" generation for nothing.

The older generation is, generally, a humble one. Some think it's vain to write about their lives. The boomers have no such qualms. They are more introspective; they think about their lives and what their purpose has been, whether they have made a difference, and whether they have lived the life they wanted. Why the heck did they take that job, or move there, or marry that person?

Baby boomers are more likely to admit mistakes too, and chalk them up as just another step in the journey to self discovery. The prevalence of tell-all memoirs, talk shows, and reality TV shows reflects an attitude of acceptance, openness, and candor. Baby boomers are approaching their later years and deaths with the same intense focus on themselves with which they live their lives. They're planning their own funerals — celebrations of life — right down to the music, flowers, and what they want done with their remains. They want to be remembered — and celebrated — for who they really are.

2.5b The boomers' parents

Many of the older generation first get prodded into doing their personal histories by their adult children. Boomers today want to know their parents' and grandparents' stories, and not only because they're also their own stories. Boomers are the privileged generation, and they know it. They're honoring their elders for their sacrifices in giving their children comfortable lives, university educations, lessons galore, and trips abroad. The younger generation wants to appreciate and understand what it's like to fight a war, immigrate to a new country, or help to build a railroad. They want to get a sense of what desperation and hunger feel like — things many have never experienced.

Boomers want everything for their kids, too. Now that people are recording every waking minute of their children's lives (including ultrasound images!), a huge piece of the puzzle would be missing if they didn't also give them their roots and family history. Boomers are the Sandwich Generation, that is, they are between their parents, who are elderly and dying, and their children, who are quickly growing up. If those from the older generation aren't documenting their lives for the family history book, it's up to them. They are the storykeepers, the link between generations, feeling a yearning to preserve and pass down their parents' experiences.

The problem is, most people are just way, way too busy. They lack the time and the knowledge to get it done.

Solution? Hire a professional.

Baby boomers are not shy about asking and paying for help when they need it. They are the generation that hires personal trainers, personal chefs, and personal shoppers. Why not a personal historian to make sure those family stories aren't lost forever?

Boomers are the largest, wealthiest demographic in history. Many have made a lot of money in the dot-com and real estate markets, and are inheriting vast pockets of wealth. They're used to paying a premium for top-quality items, especially unique items. David Foot, an economist at the University of Toronto and the author of *Boom, Bust & Echo*, predicts this huge demographic wave will be looking for products and services that are person-to-person rather than electronic or online. They will buy products that project history and quality of life. And they will see value in products that boost memory and brain power. A "biographer for hire" who can help them document and preserve their life stories will cater to all those demands.

2.5c Benefits for the storyteller

Many older people don't have a family member asking them to do their personal histories; they take the initiative themselves. They hire personal historians because they are motivated to tell their stories, put things in perspective, and leave something tangible and permanent that will be around long after they're gone.

Probably very few are aware that studies and surveys are proving that life review and reminiscence is great for health and well-being. Telling your life story, found the late Robert Butler, a Pulitzer-prize winning author renowned for his studies of healthy aging, has definite benefits, such as these stated in *Transformational Reminiscence: Life Story Work* by John Kunz and Florence Gray Soltys (Springer Publishing, 2007): " … finding meaning in life, improving problem-solving skills, assisting with the grief process, increasing emotional support, strengthening self-esteem, decreasing depression and anxiety … " Personal historians witness these changes firsthand as clients report a sense of completion and newfound peace and contentment. The process of telling your life story is usually extremely satisfying for the narrator.

3. Genealogy and Personal History

Genealogy is not quite the same as personal history, at least the way I refer to personal history in this book. Genealogists research details and facts about deceased relatives to trace the family ancestry, while personal historians tell the stories of those who are still alive to tell the tale! You might say that genealogists answer the where, who, and when questions, while personal historians have the luxury of asking a living, breathing person the why, how, and what questions. Genealogists and personal historians have traditionally lived in separate camps, but both are beginning to realize they have a lot in common and are borrowing tips and techniques from each other. The result is family history projects with more depth, detail, and appeal.

3.1 How a personal historian can work with a genealogist

Genealogists, both professional and hobbyists, are uncovering vast amounts of historical data, largely thanks to the Internet and more sophisticated searching techniques. But all too often, once they've uncovered the names, dates, charts, and documents, that's where it ends. The piles of paper are not all that accessible for sharing. They're not even that interesting, especially to the younger generation. Enter the captivating power of story. A personal historian can write a narrative that brings life to that material, illustrating it with images of maps, newspaper clippings, etc., that tells the story behind those dear departed relatives and the places and times they lived.

By the same token, personal historians can enhance their projects using the tools in a genealogist's toolbox. Besides adding important background information, research can trigger more memories, verify guesses about where ancestors settled, flesh out details about an ocean voyage, and uncover other details that add depth and context to a person's memoir. These can include:

- maps — both historic and current — about places the narrator mentions, or that illustrate a person's or family's migration over the years

- wills, birth and death certificates, military papers, census pages, passenger records

- family trees that clarify relationships

Linda Coffin, a Minneapolis, Minnesota, personal historian with extensive training and experience in genealogy, shares this example of how she used genealogy tools to enhance a personal history project:

"An elderly client wanted to know more about her mother's Polish Catholic family. Since her Polish grandfather cut off her mother for marrying an English Protestant, she doesn't have any leads. We started with the census, which shows the structure of her mother's family, listing the grandfather and grandmother as a young couple with three children. A World War I draft registration database gives her a physical description of her grandfather, his address in 1917, and the name of a brother who was listed as a family contact. City directories provide address listings for both the grandfather and his brother. Since the draft card also lists the grandfather's employer, business records can provide more information on his occupation. A search of the Catholic parish records for that part of the city opens a gold mine of information on baptisms, marriages, and burials. Land records show that the grandfather eventually moved to another state and died there. Ultimately, the client has a reunion with her second cousins — the grandchildren of the brother named on the draft registration card."

Personal historians can do some genealogical research themselves, starting with websites such as Ancestry.com/.ca, NARA.com (National Archives), and Rootsweb.com, as well as regional and local historical societies. However, hiring a professional genealogist, which can be found through the Association of Professional Genealogists at www.apgen.org, might save time and guarantee a more productive search. They are trained and experienced in using many types of repositories (archives or places of storage and preservation), and they know how to look for specific information in the right places.

Many have special areas of expertise: documents such as court records, vital records or passenger records. Others specialize by locality, such as German research, or research in Pennsylvania. Others are experts in certain repositories such as the Family History Library in Salt Lake City, or the National Archives in Washington, D.C.

If genealogy is your passion and you want to learn more, the National Genealogical Society (www.ngsgenealogy.org) offers a 16-month intensive correspondence course.

The Family History Library in Salt Lake City, the Allen County Public Library in Fort Wayne (Indiana), the Newberry Library in Chicago, Stamford University in Birmingham (Alabama), and the National Archives in Washington DC have frequent workshops and ongoing classes. The University of Toronto offers several online Certificates in Genealogical Studies with specialization in various countries.

4. Ten Essential Things You'll Learn from This Book

If you've been reading from page 1, you'll have an idea of what personal historians do and whether this is something you might seriously consider. Here are ten essential things you'll learn from this book to help you start and run your personal history business:

- The personal historian's toolkit: what you need to succeed

- Who your clients are

- Where to find clients

- How to price your product for profit

- Finding your niche

- Communicating the value of your services

- How to market yourself
- Tips for the introvert: you *can* do sales *and* public speaking
- The best resources for ongoing education
- The art of listening: a primer on interviewing (the heart of personal history)

5. Summary

The field of memoirs, family history, and preserving history is becoming more sophisticated. Digital photography, technology, and the Internet have made it easier to create and unearth the raw material — genealogical information and family trees, scans of old photographs, etc. — but often, the material sits unorganized and in danger of being forgotten and scattered. One solution is to hire a professional to help properly preserve these family stories and photographs and present them in a way that is attractive and accessible for future generations.

Technology is speeding up communication but making us hungry for meaningful connections. We need to hear the stories of our ancestors, parents, and ourselves, and we're realizing the need to preserve them permanently.

When it comes to the "close to the heart" issues of family values and heritage, people are willing to pay a premium for a high-quality product that reflects their individuality and character. The typical customer is in the mid- to upper-income bracket.

Busy baby boomers are likely to hire a professional who has the skills, experience, and time to interview themselves or older family members to capture their stories.

The core values of this business — love, living life to the fullest, memories, family, heritage, and history — hold immense appeal for boomers and their parents. These values will never go out of style and will weather recessions and economic downturns.

Though the values are timeless, the timing couldn't be better for a business that's about family values, personal fulfillment, a holistic approach to aging, connecting generations, and preserving history.

2
THE BUSINESS OF PERSONAL HISTORY

1. What You Need to Know about Being a Personal Historian

Whether you're an entrepreneur with big plans, or a second career part-timer following a life-long interest, a personal history business can be both lucrative and deeply satisfying personally and professionally. In this chapter we'll look at who typically becomes a personal historian and what being in the business entails.

1.1 Suitable backgrounds and interests

Personal historians come from all walks of life. They are writers, editors, teachers, graphic designers, photographers, genealogists, historians, memoir coaches, journalists, broadcasters, psychologists, lawyers, nurses, doctors, social workers, life coaches, anthropologists, sociologists, hospice volunteers, therapists, gerontologists, religious leaders — or anyone with an interest in preserving life stories, family histories, corporate histories, community histories, and organizational histories. Here are a few examples of how various professionals could transfer their skills to a personal history business:

- Creative-writing and memoir-writing teachers at colleges, universities and online: You're already teaching the basics and making the contacts. Why not learn how to turn these into a financially rewarding business?

- Writers, editors, journalists, and broad-casters: Bring interviewing, writing, and editing skills to draw people out to share their life stories.

- Counselors, psychologists, psychiatrists, health care workers, and gerontologists: Use listening skills and understanding of the human psyche to help people review and make sense of their lives.

- Genealogists: Add the stories behind the family tree.

- Scrapbookers and photobook publishers: A personal history business takes you a step further into the realm of the stories behind the photos.

- Other professionals who work with retirees or in any aspect of eldercare: Recent surveys and research show that reviewing one's life is highly beneficial mentally and emotionally, especially for the elderly. Related activities and programs are growing in number all across North America, at assisted living centers and seniors' residences, on tours, and at retreats, etc. The number of people involved in eldercare will grow exponentially as baby boomers get older.

1.2 Age

This is a career for someone of any age. However, it is especially appealing to those 45 and older who can relate more closely to their clients' experiences, and whose circles of contacts probably includes the target market of 50-plus. It's an ideal second career.

1.3 Solo or partners

Running a personal history business could work very well for two or more people sharing resources and the workload. The Internet, email

communication, and file-sharing make it possible for each partner to have their own office, where regular face-to-face collaboration and strategizing will produce the backbone of the business. One person could provide skills and experience in, say, marketing and outreach, while the other concentrates on the editorial work.

1.4 A family affair

Many husband-and-wife teams draw on their diverse strengths to run personal history businesses. And many personal historians employ sons and daughters for a variety of tasks, from transcribing to proofreading to scanning. The kids get the training and money, and the parent gets work done at a reasonable rate. This can be a wonderful intergenerational family business.

1.5 Five really great things about a personal history business

Here are five wonderful things about personal history businesses:

- The personal history business has very low overhead.

- Your office can be anywhere in the world. This is a highly mobile profession. It's entirely possible to spend a few months in the sun belt helping snowbirds with their memoir projects.

- The work is soul-satisfying, important, and has a lot of variety. I love the thought of the narrator's great-grandchild taking a book from his or her bookshelf and reading about an ancestor's life and times. Helping preserve something so enduring, and historically important that it becomes a family treasure ... you can't ask for a better way to make a living.

- There are few barriers. Starting and running a personal history business doesn't require formal education or training. This book is as complete a source as you will find. Experience is the best teacher and the skills required can be learned: interviewing, writing, editing, marketing and sales, etc. Anyone willing to learn and work hard can have their personal history business up and running within three months.

- You are on the cusp of an industry that's still young and has limitless potential. Now is the time to establish yourself as an expert and "catch the wave."

2. Is This Right for You?

Here are some considerations when deciding if a personal history business is the right business for you.

2.1 Work preferences

You may have taken a career assessment quiz that identifies your core personality traits as they apply to an ideal career. Some of these quizzes determine whether you're better suited to a job that deals primarily with people, information, or ideas. I think a personal historian has to want to deal with all of them. Here are the traits essential to a personal historian:

2.1a People-oriented

From my own experience and from what I've observed, a personal historian must definitely enjoy dealing with people. From the moment you first discuss a project, you establish a relationship with your client that could last a couple of years. And, people being human, a relationship has its ups and downs. Any relationship requires sensitivity, empathy and compromise. The client and business-owner relationship takes that to a whole new level.

2.1b Information-oriented

A personal historian must also like gathering information. This is done primarily through first-hand accounts from your client, but you will also find yourself doing a lot of research. Having an interest in and knowledge of history is essential. Also essential is an attention to detail, not only in the stories you'll be recording, but in the finished product. If you're creating a product that you want to last for generations, you need to make sure it's letter perfect by checking facts and figures, proofreading diligently, and working with subcontractors for quality control.

2.1c Idea-oriented

A personal historian's work involves a lot of creativity. As you listen to your clients' stories, you'll be thinking of how to make the stories as interesting and meaningful as possible. When it comes to editing and organizing the material, you'll be shaping the whole manuscript into a flowing narrative, thinking of how all the puzzle pieces fit together or how you could give the story more impact by structuring it this way or that way. Even if you hire a graphic designer to execute your ideas, it's up to you to provide the creative vision of the finished product. Of course, you can let your imagination soar as you think of all the ways to preserve history in any format.

Quiz 1 will help you decide if your skills and temperament are right for this business.

2.2 Financial circumstances

Assuming you're working from home and you have a spouse, partner, and/or children, it's important that everyone understands how important your business is to you. Ideally, they will be in full support and encourage you. If not, you have some challenges ahead, but they're not insurmountable.

QUIZ 1: PERSONAL ASSESSMENT

Take this assessment quiz to see how well you match up with the desirable qualities and skills of a personal historian:

- ❑ When I have a lot of priorities, I'm able to distinguish between what's important and what's urgent.
- ❑ I'm open-minded and nonjudgmental.
- ❑ I'm not easily discouraged.
- ❑ I'm generally an upbeat person with a positive, "let's get it done" attitude.
- ❑ I like doing new things and would get bored with the same routine every day.
- ❑ I like meeting new people.
- ❑ I'm curious about people's lives and not too shy to ask pointed personal questions.
- ❑ I can quickly regain composure when faced with emotionally charged or difficult situations.
- ❑ I have excellent interviewing skills.
- ❑ I'm good at public speaking or I'm willing to *get* good.
- ❑ I have good communication skills.
- ❑ I'm an excellent listener.
- ❑ My writing and editing skills are above average.
- ❑ I'm interested in history.
- ❑ I'm detail-oriented.
- ❑ I have some business savvy; I'm aware of good business practices.
- ❑ I'm okay with marketing myself.
- ❑ I'm self-disciplined.
- ❑ I enjoy working on my own.
- ❑ I have a support group and an alliance network.
- ❑ I'm interested in building a business, not a hobby.
- ❑ I'm patient. I'm in this for the long haul and won't give up until I've exhausted every bit of my own personal resources.
- ❑ Taking a risk and giving up a steady paycheck are not as scary to me as the thought of working for someone else all my life.
- ❑ I'm willing to make sacrifices as I get my business up and running.
- ❑ I'm good at delegating tasks and explaining what I need done and when.

How did you do? Now that you've taken a personal inventory, start planning to work on those areas you identified as ones in which you need help.

If you're employed outside the home now, try to lay the groundwork for your business before you quit, and make a realistic plan for finally kissing that job goodbye and doing what you want to do. Start saving now. If you're laid off and get a severance package, get some advice from an accountant or financial planner about how much you can safely put aside for your business start-up. The beauty of a personal history business is that there can be very little start-up cost. But you still want to have some cash put away for those rainy days when you have no clients on the horizon and the basement starts leaking.

As in any business, it may be a while before you start to see a tidy profit. There will be a learning curve where you might not be charging as much as you will once you've got some experience and a reputation. If a partner or spouse can carry you through lean times, great. But if you're on your own or you need to contribute to the household cash flow, you might want to have an alternate income stream or at least a financial cushion. You'll spend money on a leap of faith and tell yourself it's an investment, not an expense (you've heard that one before, right?). That's true, but there will be times when you might feel guilty and foolish for "wasting" your family's money. My advice: Don't!

It took me a long time to realize that in order to make money you have to spend money. I think this is a misguided mindset of a first-time businessperson. After decades of having everything supplied to you by an employer — paper, pens, computers with all the bells and whistles, and a technician to do the upgrades — one day you're looking around for some staples and you realize you have to go and buy them! When I was starting out, I told myself I wouldn't spend any money until I got my first client. I passed up the chance to attend a personal historian conference because I wasn't making any money yet and it seemed like such an extravagance. It was expensive, but I'm convinced that had I gone, I would have learned so much and made valuable connections; it would have been a very wise investment. I would have really kick-started my business, rather than having it cough and choke as it sputtered to life.

If you're leaving a job and a regular salary, there will be some financial sacrifices for a while. If you have a spouse or partner, have a frank and open discussion about finances; about your initial investment in your business, your goals, and what the next steps are if you don't meet them. The key is to set realistic expectations, set your priorities, tighten the household belt, and (keeping the analogy) buckle down and work hard to meet your goals.

If you have children, explain to them what having your own business means to you and why you're doing it. The belt-tightening might mean they don't get the latest and greatest gadget, or that Mom or Dad has to work late. Kids are far more resilient than we give them credit for, and the lessons you teach them by building your own business will stay with them throughout their lives, long after the latest gadget gives out! Involve them in helping you set up your office or doing some simple tasks. If they're older, you can increase their responsibilities and pay them hourly (or even a salary). Check with your tax accountant for the implications of adding any part-time employees.

2.2a Working at home

Get everyone to pitch in to help keep the house running smoothly. Try to set aside blocks of time when you cannot be interrupted — an office with a door is a wonderful thing!

Working at home is, I think, the best of both worlds, especially if you have children. When your children are young, you can be there for them when they need you, and you just never know when they're going to need you. Kids' needs can't be scheduled. Try as best you can to juggle things during these precious years. Ask for help when you need it. Take a break. Compartmentalize. When you're working, focus on that and that alone. When you're with your children, forget work.

The drawback to working at home is that the lines get blurred between work and home life. It's up to you to set limits.

2.3 Times of trial and tribulation

If you're in the middle of a major life change, like a divorce, moving house or renovating, having a baby, coping with a medical crisis, or caring for an elderly parent or grandparent, it's going to be very difficult to handle everything unless you have some kind of superpower. Running your own business takes an extraordinary amount of commitment, time, discipline, and sacrifice. The laundry will pile up. Friends will get brief emails instead of lengthy lunches. With some help and understanding, those things can wait. A seriously ill child or parent (or you!) cannot. Be realistic about how far you can stretch yourself at this particular time in your life.

2.4 Lifestyle considerations

Decide whether this is a part-time business or a full-time business. Think realistically about how many hours you want to work, realizing that much of the time you spend "working" will not yield direct income; you'll be marketing, taking care of administrative tasks, buying supplies, etc.; all necessary for business, but you won't get paid for them.

Also think about how much time you can spend in the evenings and weekends for networking events and maintaining relationships that will benefit your business. Is it worth it to you? You have to take into account all the demands on your time, then prioritize.

2.4a Say "no"

As a small-business owner, time is your most valuable asset. You might have been an active volunteer or participant with a church group, hospital auxiliary, theater group, choir, fundraiser, or on other noble and interesting pursuits, but there are only 24 hours in the day. Do you really enjoy the weekly book club? Can you let go of either the rowing team or the hiking group? Starting and running a business takes a lot of time and you need to say "no" to activities that don't provide you with solid networking possibilities. I can imagine you protesting, but realize that this is probably a temporary situation. Just think carefully about how you want to spend your spare time. At this juncture in your life, your priorities should be your well-being, your family, and your business. (You decide on the order!)

2.4b Say "yes"

Do what you have to do to do what you love. If you love this work, don't let anything or anyone stop you from doing it. You hate sales meetings? Get some training so you're totally comfortable talking about yourself and your products. You've been asked to speak at the local Rotary club, but the thought of public speaking makes you shake? Join Toastmasters, or just get out there and slay your dragons of fear. Feel overwhelmed at trying to keep your bookkeeping up-to-date? Spend the money and hire some help. There are very few things that can stop you from succeeding, unless you let them.

2.4c Stay positive

Stay away from negative people. You know the ones: They're skeptical and disapproving of just about anything under the sun. They complain about everything yet they never do anything to change things. In subtle or not-so-subtle ways, they'll get their message across: "Why are you being so foolish?" "Why don't you get a real job?" "Must be because you can't cut it in the corporate world!" They may resent and downplay your courage and success and suggest it's just a matter of sheer luck that you are doing well. Cut these small-minded people out of your life. Save your breath and energy for those who support you because they love you. Keep the faith. Believe wholeheartedly that this will work and it likely will.

2.4d Don't bore people!

Personal history is a fascinating field, and most people will love hearing about your work. But catch yourself if you find you're talking too much about it. You will probably get a little obsessive. After all, it is fascinating, you've invested a great deal of time and effort, and you're probably emotionally tied to it. It's your baby! But … you know the stereotypical grandmother who pulls out 40 pictures of her grandchildren and tells you about every one of their dance recitals or hockey games? Or the bore at the party who goes on and on about the boss and coworkers you don't even know? Don't expect everyone to be enthralled with your new venture. People may not have the slightest interest in it, as impossible as that might seem to you. You might find even your closest friends don't take your business seriously and treat it as another one of your hobbies or passing interests. Compartmentalize. You'll soon get to know who you can talk "shop" with, and remember, it's a two-way street. Show interest in other people's businesses and they'll probably do the same for you.

3. Terms You Should Know

In this book, I use "personal history," "memoir," "biography," and "life story" interchangeably as they all mean an account of one's life or a segment of that life. They can refer to something written by the person himself or herself, or written by someone else about the person. Here are some definitions of a few terms with which you should be familiar.

- **Autobiography**: A detailed, factual account of one's life written by oneself; more likely to be about the person's entire life; may or may not include reflection, opinions, or feelings.

- **Biography**: A life story written by someone other than the subject.

- **Corporate/Business history**: The history of a company, from its roots to present time. May include interviews with employees, leaders, customers, or people living in the community where the business operates.

- **Family history**: The story of a family that may include several generations and many branches of the family tree. May be a written account, as in a book, with photographs, or a multimedia DVD. May include interviews with one or more family members.

- **Genealogist**: A person who traces family lineages back through the generations.

- **Legacy letter/ethical will**: A document, sometimes handwritten and of any length, that expresses what the subject wants his or her loved ones to know: the lessons the subject learned from life; his or her beliefs, values and guiding principles; blessings for loved ones; advice for living a good life … whatever the subject wants to pass on to future generations. See Chapter 15 for more on ethical wills and legacy letters, and Sample 17 for samples of ethical wills.

- **Life story**: An account of a person's life. May include information about ancestors. It can be a blend of events (e.g, In 1965 I joined the firm of …) as well as reflection (e.g., In retrospect, it probably wasn't such a good idea …).

- **Life review**: Reflecting on the experiences of one's life. A term coined by a pioneer in the field, Dr. Robert Butler.

- **Memoirs**: Written reminiscences, stories, or memories about one's life or a portion of it. A memoir likely includes a good amount of reflection (how the subject remembers events as opposed to factual reenactments, and might be selective memories). There is no obligation to include details like dates, times, places, or names.

- **Personal history**: The history of a person preserved in a manuscript, book, audio or video CD or DVD, or handwritten format. The medium can vary but the objective is the same: to capture a life story, however the teller wants to tell it.

- **Oral history**: The audio or video recording of interviews of firsthand accounts of the past, generally preserved for historical importance, and generally including the transcript of the interviews. Before the written word became popular and history was written by the educated or elite groups in society, the oral tradition was the way history was passed down through time. It was revived most notably with the Federal Writers' Project in the US, in the late 1930s and 1940s, to elicit and save the stories of the diverse working-class population.

- **Reminiscence**: Remembering past experiences and events.

- **Reminiscence Therapy (RT)**: Discussion of past events and experiences usually with the aid of verbal encouragement, photographs, music, scent, memorabilia, etc. Some studies have shown RT to be beneficial for people with dementia or other memory loss, boosting self-esteem and relieving depression and promoting peace, wholeness, validation, and self-acceptance.

- **Social History**: Details about what was going on in the world and in everyday life of everyday people, from war to the price of eggs.

3
GETTING STARTED

1. The Entrepreneurial Attitude: Are You a Pair of Hands or a Visionary?

The first thing you need to decide is whether you want to find some jobs that pay the bills or whether you're starting a business. What's the difference? It's mainly one of attitude.

On one end of the work spectrum is the "pair of hands." These people are willing to follow directions and execute the vision of someone else. They don't want the responsibility or the risk of running their own business; they can forget about work at the end of the shift. Is this you? Are you satisfied to get paid for a job knowing that the person paying you is probably making money off your efforts? There's nothing wrong with that, but that's not the mindset of an entrepreneur.

Entrepreneurs want to be in control of their financial future. They want to reap the rewards of their own work and are willing to commit to making their dreams come true. They have a vision of what the business could be in a year or two or five, and they accept that they'll have to do a lot of grunt work and learn all aspects of running a business. They tend to be leaders. They have enough confidence in their abilities and their products to patiently but assertively build a clientele, and carve out a lucrative niche for themselves in the marketplace.

One more word about attitude: There's a big difference between wanting something and making it happen. Ideas are a dime a dozen. They are meaningless without action. Turn your ideas and your dreams into reality by setting real, attainable goals for yourself and your business. What do you want out of life? What do you want out of your work? Go out and get it.

2. Start Here; Get There

In this chapter we'll start building the foundation for your personal history business. My suggestions are designed to advance your core knowledge about the broad field of personal history and memoirs. When you finish reading this book and follow up with some of the suggested resources, you should be comfortable talking to potential clients. You can apply what you learn to your own particular area of interest and build a meaningful, rewarding business.

2.1 Total immersion: Absorb as much as you can about the field

Search your library and the Internet for "personal historian," "memoir writer," "business histories," "corporate histories," "oral history," "memoirs," "family history," whatever your interest. You'll find enough information to keep you reading for weeks. Bookmark especially useful sites.

2.1a Associations

There are dozens, if not hundreds, of associations and groups from which you can learn. Here are a few to get you started:

Association of Personal Historians (APH)

The mission statement, from the website www.personalhistorian.org, is "The APH is a not-for-profit international trade association. The purpose of the Association is to advance the profession of helping individuals, organizations, and communities preserve their histories, memories, and life stories. APH focuses on providing educational, training, and networking opportunities to help professional personal historians, from beginners to advanced, build

their personal history businesses." The APH has an active listserv where members can post questions, discuss issues, share resources and problem solve, a quarterly newsletter, educational materials, and an annual conference. (You can attend the conference without being a member, but as a member you get a discount.) Annual dues are around $200 and there are about 700 members worldwide, with most in the US. APH members work in a wide variety of media and formats. Search the member directory and check out websites of personal historians to see what they're offering and how they're pricing their products and services.

Explore Oral History Associations

There are several excellent oral history associations that you may want to join, depending on your interests. The WWW — the World Wide Web, or the wonderful window on the world — is a fountain of knowledge and inspiration. Look at the resources section on the CD-ROM for a list of oral history associations, or just search on Google.

The websites for these associations, some connected with academic institutions, will give you a good idea of best practices, latest research findings, interesting projects, annual conferences, and much more, including education and training. Do a search for oral history courses and workshops. Baylor University Institute of Oral History, for instance, not only has wonderful how-to resources and a collection of oral histories on its website, but it runs workshops on how to conduct an oral history. Countless other sites have fascinating recordings, such as firsthand accounts by former slaves, immigrants, Holocaust survivors, people who founded towns and businesses, First Nations and Native Americans, and just about every facet of society around the world. What a treasure chest we are building!

2.1b Institutions and ongoing projects

Stories are being gathered all over the world. This list is just a sample of the hundreds of institutions and projects devoted to preserving the personal histories and reminiscences of everyday people and specific groups:

- **The Memory Project:** This project collects firsthand accounts and digitized artifacts and memorabilia of WWII veterans. It is an initiative of the Historica-Dominion Institute, a Canadian charitable organization that promotes the history, heritage, and stories of Canada.

- **Pier 21:** Canada's Immigration Museum in Halifax, Nova Scotia, has an informative, interesting website, and the museum itself is a fascinating place to visit. Between 1928 and 1971, more than 1.5 million immigrants, war brides, displaced people, evacuee children, and Canadian military personnel passed through its doors. Pier 21 has a wonderful collection of more than 2,000 stories, 600 oral histories, books, films, photos, and documents about the immigration experience and WWII. It also offers one-on-one research help.

- **Ellis Island:** This museum in New York has extensive resources including a Family Immigration History Center. Much like Canada's Pier 21, it provides visitors with assistance in investigating "immigration history, family documentation and genealogical exploration."

- **Vermont Folklife Center:** This facility has thousands of recordings, films, photographs, and manuscripts, and on its site you can access excellent Field Guides (Digital Audio Field Recording Equipment, Field Recording in the Digital Age, Digital Editing, and Resources on Preservation).

- **StoryCorps:** This organization is part of the American Folk Life Center. It is one of the largest oral history projects, with more than 50,000 everyday people's recorded stories, many of which are recorded through the project's mobile and semi-permanent Story Booths. As described on its website, StoryCorps is " … a nonprofit whose mission is to provide Americans of all backgrounds and beliefs with the opportunity to record, share, and preserve the stories of our lives." Stories are archived in the Library of Congress. Check out the site for lots of resources including a do-it-yourself guide.

- **American Folk Life Center:** The American Folk Life Center at the Library of Congress strives to preserve folklife — "the songs we sing, the stories we tell, the crafts we make." It is home to StoryCorps (above) and the Veterans History Project, which "collects, preserves, and makes accessible the personal accounts of American war veterans."

- **Family History Centers:** Branches of the massive Family History Library in Salt Lake City, run by the Church of Latter-Day Saints, Family History Centers offer free assistance to locate ancestors, and their website, www.familysearch.org, has online resources and classes. It will be mainly of interest to genealogists, but it's an organization you should be familiar with.

2.1c Join a memoir-writing group or take a workshop

Check local institutions such as the library, university, or college to see if they offer memoir-writing classes. You might also find local groups that get together to offer support and feedback. There are hundreds (if not thousands) of memoir-writing retreats, online courses, and distance education opportunities that will coach you in the art and craft of memoir writing. "But wait," you say, "I don't want to write my own memoir!" To which I say, "How can you help other people tell their life stories or write their memoirs if you haven't experienced it yourself?" It will be enormously valuable to your work helping others, plus you'll have your life story documented for all time.

Also, if you plan to teach or lead memoir-writing classes or workshops, you'll definitely want to take one yourself to see how the instructor taught the material, what worked and what didn't, what you'd do differently, and what you can emulate in your own courses. (More on leading workshops in Chapter 15.)

2.1d Magazines and newspapers

Read newspapers, or at least scan headlines for items about personal history, memoirs, memory, storytelling, life-review programs for the elderly, etc. Go to the library and look at magazines for writers, genealogists, and family historians. Scour newspapers and the Internet for upcoming events.

2.1e Read the genre

Read memoirs and biographies. Your clients are more likely to be "ordinary" people than celebrities, but any well-written memoir will give you a sense of what makes interesting reading. Memoirs can often have all the elements of a good novel or any type of good writing: tension, resolution, believable characters, a vivid setting, dramatic arcs, and an interesting narrative voice. As you read, make your own list of things that you think make a good memoir, and make note of what resonates with you so that you can make recommendations to your clients.

Read a few business histories, even if you don't plan on offering them initially.

Read how-to guides — both books and websites — about telling your life story, writing other peoples' stories, capturing family histories, scanning photos and, if you plan to do your own design, some good books on layout and graphic design. Even if you don't plan to do your own design, you need to be able to understand the language, and what goes into good design. Go to the library and browse for books with attractive, appealing layouts.

Read books and magazines and do Internet research about working with the elderly, life review and reminiscence, and memory. "Active aging" is gaining more and more attention as our society gets older, and you'll find a lot of material that will help you understand how memory works. Some groups to explore include The International Institute for Reminiscence and Life Review, American Association of Retired People (AARP), the Canadian Association of Retired People (CARP), the U.S. National Library of Medicine, and the National Institutes of Health's MedlinePlus website.

3. Business Research and Preparation

3.1 Know thy market

If you already know what products and services you'll be offering, do some preliminary research into your target market. In a typical personal history project, you'll be capturing and preserving the life story of an older person (the narrator), but your initial contact might be in his or her 40s or 50s. You'll have to familiarize yourself with both these market segments. Read about self-publishing and learn how it is done (for more on this topic, see *Self-Publishing 101*, also published by Self-Counsel Press). There is much more information about marketing in Chapter 9.

Whatever your niche — wedding books, corporate histories, etc. — start to think about how you can sell your services.

3.2 Brush up on or learn computer skills

You will probably spend more time with your computer than you ever thought imaginable. It will be your hub for writing and editing in Word, doing accounting or number-crunching in Excel, emailing current and potential clients, researching, checking facts, scouting out potential leads, and much more.

3.3 Create a mini mission statement (by writing down your goals)

Take a few moments to write down why you want to do this work. What are your motivations? Why do you think you'll succeed? What are your short-term and long-term goals? Do you want to build a real business, or is this a one-shot deal for a specific project, like writing the history of your town or community? Write one or two paragraphs that capture your vision. (For more about mission statements and business plans, see Chapter 4.)

3.4 Check out potential competition

Ask friends and family if they know anyone who has done a family history book or memoir. Ask at the library, historical society, and genealogical society if they know any local people who provide this service. Search the library for self-published family histories or local histories, and take note of who wrote them, designed them, and published them. Take every opportunity to ask people if they have any interest in doing their memoirs or capturing their parents' or grandparents' stories. At this stage you're just trying to get a sense of general interest and elicit responses like, "Oh, Ruth Jones hired someone to do that for her mom. I'll get the name for you."

3.5 Set up your office

Start planning your special space. For now, you need to decide whether you'll work from home or rent office space elsewhere. There are pros and cons to both. Working from home is free — assuming you have room for an office and don't have to build an addition — and convenient, and gives you a lot of flexibility. You can work around children's schedules, appliance repair people, deliveries, or other commitments that require you to be home. Of course, distractions are ever-present and you need a lot of self-discipline to ignore them and get on with your work. An advantage of a home office is that you can use a portion of your expenses such as mortgage payments and utility costs as tax deductions. (Of course, you could also write off the cost of an outside office, plus your travel expenses.) If you decide to work at home, make sure your office is quiet and away from the hubbub. It doesn't have to be fancy, but it does need to be yours. This is something you'll probably want to discuss with your family.

3.6 Start spreadin' the news

It's not too early to tell friends, family, neighbors, former co-workers (and current coworkers if you have another job) that you're going to offer personal history services. You might find that you get your first client from this casual announcement! Start keeping track of names and email addresses of potential clients.

4
BUSINESS FOUNDATIONS

1. Branding: Finding the Essence of Your Company

Developing your brand can be great fun. Your business is an extension of you, so get those creative juices flowing and put your own special stamp on it. Send a message to the world: "I'm the one to call."

1.1 What is a brand?

Your brand is your image. It's what makes your business unique; what distinguishes it from the competition. It includes your business name, tagline, logo, and colors — all working together to capture the essence of your company. When your dazzling smile and captivating elevator speech can't be there, your brand is your first impression — and you know what they say about first impressions. They're lasting impressions. You only get a few seconds to spark interest in your business. Make those seconds count.

1.2 Business name

The right name can make or break a company. It can attract customers, it can turn them off, or it can be totally forgettable. A word or phrase is a lot more than just a bunch of letters strung together. A name carries all kinds of connotations and conjures up pictures and feelings in the minds of the customer. Before deciding on a business name, you have to understand who your target market is, then come up with a name that sends the right message.

Once you've brainstormed and have a list of potential business names, do a survey and try out the names. Ask people to give you their immediate, honest, gut reaction. What do they first think of when they hear your potential business name?

Try your name out on a large sample of people, though, because you will come across some biases. Everyone reacts differently to words based on their own perceptions, which in turn are based on their experiences. Take, for example, a company called Show It Off. Some people will imagine positives like "pride," "beauty," or "shiny." Others will imagine negatives like "vain," "pompous," or "accusing." We can't control how people react to certain words or phrases, so take that into account. However, we can take steps to ensure that our business name isn't offensive or projecting a negative image to the majority of people. And, needless to say, if everyone from your uncle to the convenience store owner shakes his or her head when you try your name out, it might behoove you to go back to the drawing board.

1.2a The big picture

When considering a business name, picture it as part of your logo. Picture your business name in a particular typeface plus, possibly, a graphic image. Though I recommend you wait a couple of months before designing a logo, so that you have a chance to refine your business, you should think ahead to the big picture with your business name being an element of your logo. If you intend to have a graphic as part of your logo, will your business name go with it? For instance, Pleasant Valley Memoirs is a nice, soft, romantic sounding name, and you might want a graphic of rolling hills as part of a logo. A name such as Written in Stone Productions has a harder edge, don't you think? (A tombstone logo, anyone?)

1.2b Seven tips for choosing the right name

Here are seven tips for choosing an appropriate business name:

1. If possible, match your name to an available domain name. It's so much simpler for people to find your website if it's the same as your business name. You may not be able to do this, as the choice of domain names gets slimmer by the hour, but you never know until you try. If you do find an available domain name that you like, grab it immediately. Even if you're not 100 percent sure that you'll keep it, it's cheap insurance.

2. Decide what you want people to think about (or better yet, feel) when they hear or read your name. What image do you want to project to your target market? You'll learn more about what your target market wants when you do market research, but you probably already know what you're comfortable with. Your name should feel right to you. What do you want your business name to say about you and your company? Are you traditional? Old-fashioned and homey? Trendy, chic, or urban? Warm and fuzzy? Small-town friendly? Are you a luxury purchase?

3. Make sure it describes what you do. This may sound obvious, but a lot of people name their businesses so generically you have no idea what kind of business they are, such as ABC Enterprises. You'll want to try including a word or phrase that tells what service or product your company provides. Alternatively, or in addition, you may want to consider a call to action, telling the consumer what to do (e.g., "Write it down," or "Call now!")

4. Check to see if it is available. Search as widely as you can to see if anyone else is using the name. Do a search on Google, check on the Association of Personal Historians' website, flip through the telephone directory and Yellow Pages. You can do a business name or trademark search through a paid service, or check with your state or provincial governments to see what you need to do.

5. Choose a name that allows for growth. Your name should see you through to the future. For example, right now you may just want to focus on printed memoirs, but there may come a time when you want to offer videobiographies.

6. Make it memorable, easy to identify, and easy to pronounce. Remember the multicultural society in which we live.

7. Keep it short enough to fit on a business card.

1.3 Tagline

Your tagline is the short, catchy phrase that typically pairs up with your business name. For example, my business name is Heritage Memoirs and my tagline is "Saving Life Stories for Future Generations." Your tagline should reflect what your company does, what it stands for, and what sets it apart. This is hard to accomplish in five words or fewer, but it's worth it to come up with the best one you can. This is such valuable real estate on your business card and other marketing materials, and in advertising. A few things you could consider for a tagline:

- Talk benefits. People don't care about what you do. They care about what you can do for them.

- Talk longevity. For instance, "Serving customers since 1998" says you've been around a long time and you know what you're doing.

- Talk specialties. Go after your niche market.

- Talk expertise. Toot your horn. What makes you the logical person to hire?

- Think outside of the box and be different and creative.

- Consider a simple call to action (like Nike's "Just do it.").

- Make it catchy and clever ("I'm lovin' it," by McDonald's).

- Capture imaginations ("Where would you like to go today?" by Microsoft).

- Appeal to emotions ("Doesn't your dog deserve Alpo?" by Alpo dog food).

1.4 Logo

Your logo is the visual representation of your company. It has to have the right look and feel for the nature of your business. Companies spend millions of dollars designing logos that stand out, grab attention, and reflect who they are. Logos don't have to have graphics. Look at Coca-Cola: It has one of the most recognizable brands in the world and its logo is simply the letters of its name in a flowing script; no fancy graphics. But a graphic can help your business name stick in your customer's mind. Long after he or she forgets the name of your company, he or she might just remember an image. Whether you choose to include a graphic or not, keep your logo clean and simple.

If you can afford it, it's worth it to hire a professional (not your neighbor's son who has a flair for drawing and really needs to make some money) to help you develop brand materials, such as logo, business card, website, and brochures. If a professional's fee is just not in the budget now (it can easily cost more than $3,000), consider calling your local college or university graphic arts or marketing programs and inquiring if they have students' projects that involve real-world companies. It probably won't be free, but it should save you a chunk of money.

Tip: If you hire a designer, make sure that you receive your files in the correct formats (TIFF versus JPG) for both web and print, as formats are not interchangeable. A graphic designer should be able to advise you on this.

2. Your Business Plan

2.1 Why a business plan is essential

Like a lot of small-business owners, I resisted doing a business plan for a long time. I think it was a psychological block. Maybe it had something to do with fear of actually stating goals, because what if I didn't achieve them? Or, if I documented plans and strategies, that meant I couldn't wing it — I'd stifle my creative side! Uh-uh. It doesn't work that way. I finally got some serious business coaching, and guess what the first item on the agenda was? Do a business plan.

A business plan is valuable in so many ways. The preparatory work and research will help you learn about the industry. It will help you dream big, but will make sure you sprinkle those dreams with a healthy dose of reality. You'll compile resources that will help you when you launch your business. You may even meet potential partners and clients. The actual writing of the plan will help you clarify your thinking and force you to be specific about what you're offering and how you're going to do it.

Try this: imagine you are franchising your business. Your business plan should contain enough detail to convince potential franchisers of the great opportunity but also give them a clear, honest assessment of risks, challenges, and potential pitfalls. Another approach is to write it as an operations manual, describing the many facets of your business and how it operates. This is an excellent exercise in itself; you'll have it all written out should you one day expand and hire some help.

Further down the line, once you've been operating for a while, your business plan also allows you to monitor your progress and compare what you thought you'd be doing and what you've actually ended up doing. It should be an organic, "living" document that changes and develops as you operate your business.

2.2 Parts of Your Business Plan

Let's look at the parts of a business plan. Sample 1 shows a sample business plan template.

2.2a Company profile

This is a snapshot of your company: the who, what, when, where, and why. It should include your ownership structure — whether you're a sole proprietorship, partnership, corporation or, in the US, an LLC (Limited Liability Corporation) or an S corporation. Business legalities vary from province to province, state to state, and country to country, so check with your local business development centers and government departments. In Canada, the federal government has numerous online resources for business start-ups and small businesses, one being Canada Business (www.canadabusiness.ca). In the US, a good resource is Business.gov (www.business.gov/register/incorporation).

Three possible business structures are:

- **Sole proprietorship**: operating the business on your own, either under your own name or a business name. A sole proprietorship is owned and operated by

BUSINESS PLAN TEMPLATE

Think through and fill in each section for your business.

Your Name: _____

Name of Company: _____

Start Date: _____

Address and Phone Number: _____

Business Number (if available): _____

Structure and Type of Business:
(e.g., Mary Jane Memoirs is a sole proprietorship/partnership/corporation providing personal history services to local and regional individuals, families, communities, and businesses.)

Elevator Speech:
(i.e., the overview of your services and products in one paragraph)

Mission Statement:
(i.e., one or two sentences to describe the overall goal and purpose of your business)

Vision Statement:
(i.e., a broad, inspirational statement describing the size, structure, and influence of your business in the future; where you're headed)

Products and Services:

Industry Overview:

Key Initiatives and Objectives:

Regulatory Issues:

Risks:

Implementation Plan:
(Describe how you're going to accomplish your goals)

Financial Plan:

one person. This is the simplest business structure and probably the easiest way for you to open your business to at least get it started. It has the fewest regulations. Once you start making over a certain amount, there can be tax implications.

- **Partnership**: operating the business with one or more partners. Usually, this means two or more persons and means extra capital and expertise available in the business right away. However, there can be difficulties when you cannot just run things the way you want without checking with your partner, and vice versa. Partnerships can be viable ways to start and run businesses but contracts are recommended; in the US, consider *The Small-Business Contracts Handbook* and in Canada, see *Partnership Agreement*, both published by Self-Counsel Press, for such a contract.

- **Corporation**: operating as a separate legal entity. Corporations are legal entities, which means they are separate and distinct entities from the individuals who start them and from any other legal entities. One advantage to incorporating is limited liability; shareholders' assets are separate from business assets and cannot be seized to pay debts incurred by the corporation, for example. There are many regulations, tax implications, and things to watch out for when running a corporation. If you choose to go this route, I suggest you research how to incorporate in your area.

The major difference between a sole proprietorship and a corporation is that in a corporation, an individual is not normally responsible or liable for debts incurred by the business. If you aren't sure which is the best structure for you, consult a lawyer, accountant, or local small-business association for more information.

Your company profile also includes your business registration number, when the company was registered, when the company was started, where it will operate, and number of employees. Include a line or two about why you are in this business, what your background is, and what led you to start your company.

2.2b Your elevator speech, or 30-second commercial

The name "elevator speech" refers to the amount of time it takes to ride an elevator up a few floors; about 30 seconds or so. An elevator speech should say what you do, who you work with, and why people hire you.

Imagine yourself in the grocery store. You bump into an old acquaintance you haven't seen in a long time. "What are you doing now?" she asks. You have 30 seconds to tell her, and hopefully in a way that will impress her enough to ask about your business. Ideally, she'll think, "Gosh, that sounds like me. I've got that problem, too. Maybe Jennifer could help me."

By the way, have an answer for the follow-up question, "Oh, that sounds interesting. How much would something like that cost?" To which the answer begins "It depends." More on pricing in Chapter 5 and marketing in Chapter 9.

After you do your market research, you'll know a lot more about your customer. Right now, fill in these blanks:

1. My target client is _____.

2. He or she is facing a problem about _____ _____.

3. I can help him or her because _____ _____.

For instance, you might say,

1. *My target client is a baby boomer. Her parents are in their 80s or 90s; one of them may have recently passed away. She probably has kids of her own. She probably works outside the home.*

2. *She's facing a problem because she's afraid she's going to lose the family stories. She wants to get her parents' life story but she's overwhelmingly busy and she doesn't know how to go about it.*

3. *I can help her because I have the time and skills to capture her parents' stories and preserve them.*

Craft your own 30-second elevator pitch. Practice until its rolls off your tongue effortlessly. Write it in your business plan. Remember you can always refine it as you go along.

2.2c Mission and vision statements

Your vision statement is "blue-sky" thinking (clear, no clouds) that addresses the question: What kind of company are you? By this I mean what's your corporate culture — on what principles do you operate? What are the values of your company? If you could propel yourself 100 years into the future, how would you want your company described?

Take a minute to think about the values with which you'll run your company. They're probably not that different from how you run your life.

Your mission statement is more about your goals; what you want to do through your company. Not "make $40,000 this year," but what you're committed to, and what you strive to be. Starbucks' mission statement is: "To inspire

and nurture the human spirit — one person, one cup, and one neighborhood at a time." Disney's is "Make people happy."

My mission statement is "To help individuals, families, businesses, and organizations preserve their histories, memories, stories, and values. We will strive to provide a richly satisfying experience for the narrator and a family heirloom for future generations."

My vision statement is a lot more mushy. I talk about principles of integrity, quality, and trust, and values like family, love, tradition, and finding the meaning and purpose in life.

2.2d Products and services

Describe what you're selling, and how you do what you do. Don't know yet? You better find out soon, and here's a golden opportunity!

Describe your product. Visualize it and describe what it looks like: the size, color, weight, and packaging. Describe the features, but more importantly, the benefits — how will your product make life better for your customers? What problem will it solve for them? Now describe how you will produce it.

Regarding services, explain what people will pay you for, and how you perform the services. Answer the questions: Why should a client care? Why would someone hire you? Go into as much detail as possible and include how you'll communicate with clients, what you'll do for them, what tools and technology you'll use, and what your business hours will be.

2.2e Industry overview

Write an overview of the industry. The personal history industry encompasses many products and services, ones that are similar to yours and ones that may be complementary or supplementary. Do some exploring locally and find companies with which you might potentially share a market. Then go global with the Internet, and search for companies that do what you do. See if they advertise through Google ads or on other websites. How many and what type of companies are in your industry? Will the size of the industry expand? If so, why? What factors — the economy, demographics, your location, technology, etc. — affect the health and growth potential of your industry? How do your products and services fit into the industry? Why is there a need for your products and services?

2.2f Key initiatives and objectives

This section is the most important part of your business plan. This is where you write down specific goals. For example, how much income do you want to make in the first year, and what steps will you take to get there — that is, what marketing strategies will attract the number of sales necessary to achieve that income? Once you've set a goal of an annual income, work backward to determine what your hourly rate needs to be. (See more about pricing in Chapter 5.)

2.2g Regulatory issues

Check to see if your local government (or strata) has bylaws regarding home-based businesses. Although it's not likely that your municipality will shut you down because you didn't comply with zoning laws, it's best to do some research first. If your business meant that you had a lot of deliveries and clients were parking up and down your street, or you were running a daycare and had ten children playing on the front lawn … then your bylaws officer might have something to say about it. Some municipalities have strict bylaws against advertising on a home, or even having a commercial vehicle parked in the driveway. Check with your local authorities to set your mind at ease.

2.2h Risks

One of the best things about a personal history business is that there is relatively little start-up cost. You may already have all the equipment and office supplies you'll need. However, there are always expenses you haven't planned for, and if you're engaged in building a business, you're not making much money elsewhere. Are you prepared to invest in your business with the possibility of losing money? Is your family behind you on this? What support system do you have in place? What's Plan B?

2.2i Implementation plan

Take an hour or so to map out a timeline of how you're going to operate your business. First make a list of all you need to do, which might seem daunting or overwhelming, but not if you think in small steps. Look at your schedule for the next month, or year, and make a note of when you're going to have such-and-such accomplished. If something is dependent on something else, make a note of that.

Sample 2 is a list of things to do as you start your business. The items aren't necessarily in order. Set goals for accomplishing these tasks. As you complete them, check them off with the date of completion and how much each one cost you.

2.2j Financial Plan

A financial plan answers the questions: Where's the money going to be spent? And where's the money going to come from?

It's tentative at this point, but you need to make some assumptions and decide approximately how much you're going to charge for your products and services and how much you think you're going to sell. In your market, with your expertise and resources, is it best if you offer a lower-cost product and hope to do

SAMPLE 2
START-UP TO-DO LIST

Task:	Target Date for Completion:	Completed:	Cost:
Choose business name			
Register business name and get business registration number			
Create identity – name, logo, tagline, colors, "look and feel"			
Market research			
Business plan			
Marketing plan/ Marketing action plan			
Set up filing and organizational system			
Set up office			
Get business cards printed			
Secure a domain name and hosting and design company for website			
Write website copy			
Launch website			
Develop list of potential clients			
Set up business bank account			
Set up business phone line or change voicemail message on home phone			
Write a sales letter with your bio, services, and contact information			

Establish pricing			
Write a contract			
Set up invoicing system/create invoice template			
Check insurance needs for home office and for errors and omissions			
Set up bookkeeping system/register for GST/HST (Canada)			
Complete sample personal history project			
Research suppliers and sub-contractors; make initial contact			
Join professional development associations and networking groups			
Practice speaking elevator speech you wrote in your business plan			
Establish support/advisory group			
Create a Sales Action Plan with specific goals (e.g. make five calls per week)			

a large volume? Or will you go after just a few high-end clients? You also have to decide on things such as:

- Will you charge for travel time?

- What are your terms of payment going to be?

- Are your sales going to be seasonal?

You'll need to consider fixed and variable costs going forward. With each project, you'll have fixed costs such as paper, gas for the car, CDs — anything you're going to spend on an actual project. Above that, you'll have fixed costs such as house and car insurance, website maintenance, association or networking group membership fees, online or print subscriptions, household upkeep, meals, utilities, car repairs, communication expenses (cell, Internet, home phone), taxes, maintenance, and so on. On top of this, you may have accountant's and lawyer's fees, travel expenses, conferences and trade shows to attend, gifts to buy for clients, entertainment expenses, and on and on. If you've never done a budget, this is a great time to start. You've got to keep a realistic snapshot of your business, and in order to do that, you have to know what expenses you have. If that's not motivation to get out there and make some money, pin a picture of a villa in Tuscany — or whatever your dream is — on your bulletin board, and have a look at Sample 3, which is also available on the CD-ROM included with this book, so you can work out your expenses.

3. Legalities

3.1 Registering your business name

In the US, the legal name of a business is the name of the person (or entity) who owns the business, for instance, Mary Jane Jones. If Mary Jane wants her business name to be Mary Jane Memoirs, she needs to file a fictitious name registration form with the government agency of her state. "Fictitious name" is also known as assumed name, trade name, or "DBA" (Doing Business As) name. Check with your local authorities as to procedures in your area. Your lawyer or accountant should also be able to tell you how to register your legal business name.

In Canada, business registration is governed at the provincial level, so check with your provincial government for correct procedures. Unless you're operating a sole proprietorship under your legal name (e.g., Mary Jane Jones), you need to register your business name.

3.2 Business bank account

To open a business bank account, you will either need a Business Number (BN) in Canada or an Employer Identification Number (EIN) in the US. Check with your state or provincial government for procedures. Opening a business bank account and keeping your personal accounts separate will make accounting for your business and personal life that much simpler, and will help you avoid any potential issues should you ever be audited by the Internal Revenue Service (IRS) or Canada Revenue Agency (CRA).

3.3 Taxation issues

If you are a Canadian business owner, you are eligible to register for the GST/HST (Harmonized Sales Tax). That means you can "reclaim" some of the GST/HST you spend on business purchases. The catch? You have to register for GST/HST, and remit it to Canada Revenue Agency on a regular basis. If your total taxable revenues are $30,000 or higher, you MUST register. If they are below $30,000, you don't have to, but in most cases it's to your advantage. Whether you live in the US or Canada, taxation issues are complicated, and you should seek the advice of an experienced bookkeeper or accountant.

SAMPLE 3
FINANCIAL ASSUMPTIONS ON START-UP, FIXED AND VARIABLE OPERATING COSTS TEMPLATE

Contributed by Owner	
Computer	$2,000.00
Car	
Laptop	
Scanner	
Digital Recorder	
Office Furniture	
Lawyer	
Business Name Registration	
SUBTOTAL	$2,000.00
Direct Costs from Contracts	
Supplies	$50.00
Sub-contracting	
Transcriber	
Graphic Designer	
Client Appreciation Gifts	
SUBTOTAL	$50.00
Communications	
Website	$100.00
Internet Access	
Cell Phone	
Long Distance Charges	
Subscriptions	
SUBTOTAL	$100.00
Professional Development	
Association Memberships	
Courses	
SUBTOTAL	$0.00

Advertising and Marketing	
Supplies	
Marketing Materials	
Trade Show Signage	
Conferences	
Meals and Entertainment	$5.50
Auto Expenses	
Advertising	
Travel	
SUBTOTAL	$5.50
Home Office	
Gas	$20.00
Water	
Insurance	$114.00
Property Tax	
Mortgage	
Hydro	
Repairs and Maintenance	
SUBTOTAL	$134.00
GRAND TOTAL	$2,289.50

3.4 Get it in writing: Your legal documents

3.4a Client contract

Do not start any work on a project without a signed contract and a deposit. The best-laid plans can and do go awry for circumstances beyond anyone's control. What you can control is fair compensation for yourself.

Consider this scenario: Five weeks ago, you met with a potential client. He phoned you a week later and said, "Let's go!" You sent him a contract a month ago, and there's no forward motion in sight. In the meantime, you turned down another job because you wouldn't have had time for it because of your commitment to this first gentleman, and you did two hours of research about his family business in preparation for the interview that was supposed to happen two weeks ago. Now he's avoiding your phone calls and it looks like the project got derailed for some reason.

You don't have a client until you've got a contract. See Samples 4 and 5 for sample letters of agreement. These samples are also available on the CD-ROM included with this book for your use.

You should always consult a lawyer for the wording of your contract because laws differ from state to state, province to province, and country to country. When dealing with contracts, there are certain rights and responsibilities that need to be covered.

In your contract, outline what your responsibilities are and what your client's responsibilities are. Some of the things to consider in a contract:

- Make sure the client understands that the manuscript will be based on the interviews and be in first person. Thoroughly explain what that means. (This is misunderstood more often than you'd imagine.) Of course, if you're going to write in third person, put that in writing.

- Make sure the client understands that you are not doing a lot of research to add to the story unless you're being paid for it.

- Make it clear that you won't be held liable for factual errors provided to you by the client or his or her family.

- Copyright: Who retains copyright to the product, you or the client? If you're acting as a co-author or ghostwriter and the book might end up being commercially published or even made into a Hollywood blockbuster, you'd want to negotiate any possible future royalties. If, however, you are working as a contractor for hire and the book, CD, or DVD is in the author's own words, the work would most likely remain the copyright of the client (or narrator). This is a matter for you to decide on a project-by-project basis. For more information about copyright visit the US copyright office at www.copyright.gov or in Canada, visit the Canadian Intellectual Property Office at www.cipo.ic.gc.ca.

- Be very specific about what the final product or service is.

- Put in a clause for "variations" such as extra rounds of revision, additional travel, additional interviews, etc.

- List all inclusions and exclusions: For example, does your fee include tax? Travel time? Does it exclude photocopying or courier charges?

- Consider including a clause that states that you will receive at least one copy (at the client's expense) of the finished product and be allowed to display it as part of your portfolio. Not all clients

LETTER OF AGREEMENT
(for manuscript preparation)

This AGREEMENT between

[client name and address]

and

[personal historian name and address]

entered into this _____ day of _____ [month], _____ [year], for the purpose of establishing a mutually satisfactory arrangement whereby the rights and responsibilities of both parties are described and protected. Client engages the services of _____ [Personal Historian] in the writing and editing of a manuscript, "Project," about the life story, memoirs, or reminiscences of _____ [Narrator].

I. SERVICES: (Personal Historian) will provide the following services:

1. Preparation and Interviews:

   - Pre-interview preparation and consultation with Client and/or Narrator

   - Research

   - Question preparation

   - Up to 10 hours of recorded interviews with Narrator. Client and/or Narrator may choose to include interviews with others in the 10 hours of interviews.

2. Transcription and Editing:

   - Transcribing of the audio recordings

   - Editing, organizing the text into a cohesive narrative, re-writing where necessary, delivery of first draft of manuscript for revisions and corrections. Revisions to first draft that exceed 4 hours of Personal Historian's time will be charged at an hourly rate of _____. Delivery of final manuscript.

II. FEE FOR SERVICES: Client shall pay Personal Historian at the hourly rate of _____. It is estimated that total fee will be in the range of _____ to _____.

III. TERMS OF PAYMENT: Client shall pay Personal Historian a deposit of _____ on signing of this letter of agreement. Such amount represents ¼ of total final estimated fee.

Second Payment: Second payment (¼ of total final estimated fee) is due upon completion of interviews.

Third Payment: Third payment (¼ of total final estimated fee) is due upon delivery of first draft of manuscript.

Fourth Payment: Fourth and final payment is due upon delivery of final draft approved by Client. Amount of final payment will be adjusted to account for actual hours worked by Personal Historian.

IV. VARIATIONS: Personal Historian agrees to keep Client informed on progress of Project. Personal Historian agrees not to incur any extra costs on behalf of Project without Client's permission.

Personal Historian is willing to travel to accommodate further interviews, editing, writing or research; expenses paid by Client.

QUALITY: Client acknowledges that manuscript will be a first-person narrative based on the interviews transcribed. The Personal Historian will make every effort to ensure that facts are correct but cannot be held responsible for factual errors. Client agrees to ensure, to the best of his or her knowledge, that facts are correct upon first and second reading before final draft is delivered.

RIGHTS: Personal Historian acknowledges that the Project is a "work for hire" created within the scope of Personal Historian's employment as an independent contractor, and that the Narrator is to be considered the "author" for the purpose of copyrighting the Project. The Project created pursuant to this Agreement is intended for the private use of Client and his or her friends and family only. Notwithstanding this fee-for-hire arrangement, if Project is published and sold commercially, either in print, film or electronic media, Personal Historian shall be entitled to, and Client agrees to pay, 5% of any royalties that Client receives, and 5% of any advance on royalties, and 5% of any and all revenues resulting from any secondary or subsidiary rights granted in the Project.

Client specifically agrees to protect, indemnify and hold Personal Historian harmless from and against any loss, damage, liability or expense, including attorney's fees, due to any damage to person or property caused or alleged to have been caused by Client in connection with the operation of this agreement.

Personal Historian reserves the right to display the Project for promotion and advertising purposes as part of her portfolio.

CANCELLATION: This agreement may be cancelled by either party with two weeks written notice. Personal Historian shall be paid for all work completed up to receipt and acknowledgement of cancellation notice.

In witness whereof, the parties have executed this agreement on the day and year first above written.

Personal Historian by _____
                       (Personal Historian's name)

Client by _____
              (Client's name)

SAMPLE 5
LETTER OF AGREEMENT
(hourly rate for manuscript and book production)

This AGREEMENT between

[Client]

and:

[Personal Historian]

entered into this _____ day of _____ [month], _____ [year], and is for the purpose of establishing a mutually satisfactory arrangement whereby the rights of both parties are described and protected. Client engages Personal Historian's services in the publication of a book based on interviews about the life story, memoirs, or reminiscences of [Narrator].

SERVICES: Services provided by the Personal Historian will include but not be limited to:

- **Preparation and Interviews:** Question preparation, interviews with Client, recorded and preserved on CD.

- **Transcription and Editing/Rewriting of Recorded Interviews**: Transcribing of interviews, organizing, writing and editing text into cohesive, logical segments of Client's life story, creating chapter breaks and titles, and otherwise preparing delivery of first draft to Client, revisions according to Client's changes, delivery of final manuscript for Client approval. If requested, Personal Historian will also incorporate existing written material into manuscript and interview other people to provide third-party quotes about the Narrator. Once Client has approved the final manuscript, it will be copy-edited, proofread, and formatted to professional publishing standards, ready for publication.

- **Project Management of Book Publication:** Preparing text, photographs, and documents for printing, project management for book design and publication, and any other work related to the delivery of the book. Personal Historian will obtain Client's approval of book proofs before printing.

FEE FOR SERVICES: Client agrees to pay Personal Historian for all labor and costs, including travel time and courier charges, associated with the project, including those listed above plus any necessary research, fact-checking, consultation, and any other related work. Client shall pay Personal Historian for all services at the hourly rate of _____, billed monthly at the beginning of the month. A retainer fee of _____ is requested upon signing of this letter of agreement, which will represent payment for the first _____ hours of Personal Historian's time spent on this project.

*Appropriate taxes will be added to final invoice.

Personal Historian agrees to keep Client informed on progress of Project with regular updates.

QUALITY: Client acknowledges that manuscript will be a first-person narrative based on the interviews transcribed and material provided. The Personal Historian will make every effort to ensure factual accuracy but cannot be held responsible for factual errors.

RIGHTS: Personal Historian and Client acknowledge that the Project is a "work for hire" created within the scope of Personal Historian's employment as an independent contractor, and that the Client is to be considered the "author" for the purpose of copyrighting the Project ("work"). The Project created pursuant to this Agreement is intended for the private use of Client and his or her friends and family.

Personal Historian will receive two copies of finished book. Client grants Personal Historian the right to use the finished book as part of his or her portfolio for marketing and promotional purposes.

In witness whereof, the parties have executed this Agreement on the date of signing below.

Personal Historian by _____   _____
(Personal Historian's name)   Date

Client by _____   _____
(Client's name)   Date

will agree to this, but it's a perfectly fair request. In one instance, the personal historian was allowed to keep one copy of a client's book only until she (the personal historian) died. It was then to be returned to the client's family.

You should also consider asking your client to sign a consent form that protects you should you want to use the book, audio recording, reviews, or testimonials in any marketing materials.

Sample 6 is a consent form that addresses this issue.

3.4b Cancellation

What about cancellation? What happens if something unexpected happens, such as your client dying?

Your contract should stipulate that if the project cannot be completed for any reason, both parties will, if possible, give the other party written notice. Obviously, if the client dies, the client's family would be your contact — which is why it's important to try to get the contact information of another family member if your contract is with the narrator. In this unfortunate circumstance, the family may indeed decide to go ahead with the project if you have enough material. However, don't assume anything. In one instance when a client died, the family — astonishingly — had no interest in the client's story and did not want the manuscript a personal historian had prepared up until then. They refused to pay the personal historian for his work. So, have a clause that states you will get paid for the work you've done to date should anything happen that prevents the project from being completed. If this seems like overkill (pardon the pun), it's not. More than one personal historian has been stiffed (again, excuse me!) by unfortunate circumstances.

Protect yourself. By the same token, you should agree that, should you pass away or otherwise be prevented from completing the project, the material you've prepared so far will be returned to the client. This is one reason it's important to let someone know how to access your files and keep contact information in one place.

3.4c Indemnity

You have to protect yourself from any possible lawsuits that might result from the finished product. Sample wording might go something like: "Client agrees that Personal Historian will be held harmless from any loss, damage, liability or expense, including attorney's fees, that may arise due to any damage to person or property caused or alleged to have been caused by Client or Client's Project in connection with the operation of this Agreement."

3.4d Terms of payment

If you're working on an hourly basis, consider asking for an advance (or retainer or deposit) to cover a certain number of hours as the project begins. If your rate is $40 per hour and you think you'll be working 6 hours for each of the first two weeks, it's perfectly acceptable to ask for an advance of 12 x $40 = $480. After you've worked that 12 hours, continue to keep track of your time and send an invoice every month (or every two weeks if you choose). I don't think it's necessary to itemize each task, but some clients may want to see it broken down by types of tasks; say, interview time, editing, transcribing, etc.

If you're working on a "package price" — a total fee — your terms of payment can be by milestone such as "Deposit," "End of Interviews," "Delivery of First Draft," "Delivery of Final Manuscript and Audio CDs," etc.

CONSENT FORM

I _____ understand and accept the following conditions of this
project, _____ [title of project/proposed book title].

I give _____ [Personal Historian] permission to keep one copy of
the Project and to display that copy as a sample of his or her work. Display may include but not be
limited to public presentations the Personal Historian gives to groups, potential clients, media, and to
the Personal Historian's website.

1. Passages from this Project may be used in promotional material developed by
   _____ [Personal Historian].

   This promotional material may include letters, brochures, booklets, website copy, or spoken
   word. Distribution may include but not be limited to public presentations, potential clients,
   articles, and books written by the Personal Historian, or quotes in media interviews given by
   Personal Historian.

   ❑ I agree to be quoted directly

   ❑ I agree to be quoted anonymously

3. Personal Historian agrees to obtain permission from Client to use Client's Project for any
   commercial purpose, meaning any transaction in which money is received for the use of Client's
   project.

4. Personal Historian may quote my favorable testimonial of his or her services and this project on
   Personal Historian's website, in public presentation, interviews, and promotional material.

Client _____   _____
                    (Client's name)   Date

Personal Historian _____   _____
                    (Personal Historian's name)   Date

3.4e Invoice

When you've decided on your pricing structure (see Chapter 5 for more on pricing), look at Sample 7 for an invoice template. Here's what your invoice should include:

- Your logo and/or letterhead
- The client's name and address
- The name of the project
- The billing date
- What the payment is for
- The number of the invoice for your own record
- If you're working on an hourly basis, the number of hours worked multiplied by your hourly rate, showing the total
- If you're working on a package price, the deliverable ("First Draft," etc.) and the agreed-upon amount due
- If you need to charge tax, you can add the appropriate tax now or wait until the final invoice
- Somewhere on the invoice, perhaps at the bottom, state your payment terms: when it is due (e.g., 10 to 30 days from billing date) and charges for late payment (e.g., 2 to 8 percent per month). As a small-business owner with expenses of your own, you cannot afford to wait six weeks or two months to be paid for the work you've done. We establish close, friendly relationships with our clients, but beware of clients who become slack in paying you. Show them you are a true professional. If payment is overdue, send a reminder. If you still don't get paid, send another reminder, and charge them interest. Do you think Visa would be okay with you saying the check will be in the mail just as soon as you get paid in a couple of weeks?

3.4f Copyright/permissions release form

When publishing a book and including photographs, illustrations, or other copyrighted material, you must secure permission from the owner of the copyright. Many times, you'll only need written permission, but occasionally you might have to pay for it. If you do have to pay, be sure you collect the money from your client.

A copyright/permissions form may include wording such as the following, and may be changed depending on your needs:

I _____
(name)

of _____
_____
(address)

grant permission to

_____
(your name or name of client)

to reproduce and use my photograph/artwork _____
(identifying photo)

in a book entitled _____
_____.

It is agreed that with each use of my work I will be given credit as written: "Photograph by _____.

Used with permission."

(Signature) _____
(Name of Artist) _____
(Date)_____

INVOICE

Invoice #[7]

[Date]

[Your name and business]

[Client's name and address]

In payment for personal history services covering the period of _____ to _____.

Hours as at _____

40 hours x _____ hourly rate ....$ _____

Paid to date..$ _____

Amount due..$ _____

Payment is requested within 14 days of receipt of this invoice.

With thanks,

[Your name]

3.4g Client sign-off/approval form

The sign-off form is a "speak now or forever hold your peace" document — another way to protect yourself against damages, both financial and reputation. It states that the client agrees that the manuscript is what she wants printed and that there's no blaming you when the book is printed and she remembers Aunt Catherine actually spelled her name Katherine.

Sample 8 is a sign-off or approval form.

4. Help from Experts

4.1 Lawyer

It's wise to engage the services of a lawyer. He or she will review your contracts, advise you on partnerships and alliances, deal with copyright issues, and advise you about getting a trademark. It's well worth the money to give you confidence that you're making the right decisions and your contracts contain language that's enforceable. Not much use having anything else, is it?

4.2 Accountant

An accountant is another professional you should get acquainted with. You can receive help in many areas, such as:

- reviewing your financial plan, sales forecasts, and budgets

- advising on company structure

- setting up financial record-keeping systems

- reviewing your bookkeeper's work

- recommending computer software that will help you stay organized

- optimizing your tax deductions

- preparing your tax returns and dealing with any other issues that come your way courtesy of the Internal Revenue Service (IRS) or Canada Revenue Agency (CRA)

- remitting GST/HST or other taxes (where applicable)

4.3 Insurance agent

Talk to your insurance agent about protecting yourself and your business. Don't assume your existing home insurance or car insurance will cover business assets. It's even possible that having your business located in your home may void your regular home insurance policy. Periodically, review your insurance policies with your agent. As your business grows you might need more. Or, there could be some changes that mean you don't need as much.

He or she can help you evaluate your risks and decide on the types of coverage and the amount. Various types of insurance include:

- property theft and damage;

- client injuries (depending on where you conduct business);

- errors and omissions: You let a typo slip by on the cover of a book, it has to be reprinted, and guess who's responsible for the charges? Errors and omissions insurance can protect you in situations like this; and

- loss or damage to a client's possessions. Bear in mind that no amount of money could compensate the loss of something of great sentimental value. Whenever possible, do not remove your clients' possessions from their homes or offices.

SAMPLE 8
SIGN-OFF/APPROVAL FORM

I _____, have read the manuscript entitled _____

_____, and give my approval to publish it.

_____   _____

            [Client's name]   Date

4.4 Support groups

4.4a Advisory boards/mentors

Running a business can be daunting, but you don't have to go it alone. Through your contacts and networking, look for three or four marketing and business experts who will advise you and help you strategize every couple of months or so. Issue a written invitation outlining what you need from them and for how long (probably no longer than a year). It's best to meet in person, with a set agenda that you can send to them in advance so they know about which specific areas you'll be seeking advice. Bounce ideas off them, get their advice on a new product or service, ask about their own experiences, and generally learn as much as you can from them. Respect their time and show your appreciation. Buy them breakfast or lunch, cover their expenses, and think about giving them an honorarium for their help.

You must know and trust these people, as you'll be sharing information about your company that could potentially harm your business if it fell into the wrong hands. Ask your advisors to sign a non-disclosure agreement and a non-compete agreement.

Along the same line, but in a one-to-one relationship with someone who's already made inroads in the personal history field, find a mentor who will share his or her expertise and advice. (And in the interest of good karma, do the same for someone else once you're wildly successful.)

Where to find these angels? Besides a personal history association, many networking associations have mentoring programs. You could also try calling your local small-business center, chamber of commerce, or organization of retired executives, and ask if any local business people volunteer such services.

4.4b Mastermind groups and dream teams

Many business people, especially entrepreneurs, get together regularly with a group to brainstorm, share resources, give feedback, celebrate successes, problem solve, network, advise, challenge, and encourage each other. These are known as mastermind groups or dream teams.

Mastermind-type groups are usually a group of about eight to ten people. Membership is voluntary and free, but commitment is important. The idea behind mastermind groups is that the whole is greater than the sum of the parts; that is, the group itself is an entity with a personality and voice of its own. Members do what's best for each other and what's best for the group. There are no hard-and-fast rules, but here are a few things to consider:

- Choose your group carefully. Mutual respect and trust is important. Think about your professional circle. Who do you admire and feel a kinship with? The group can be derailed by personality clashes that waste time and drain energy; members who hog the limelight; members who are defensive or secretive; members who don't show up or arrive late.

- At your first meeting, agree on the principles of the group — that you'll meet every week at the same time, same place; there's no excuse for not attending without letting someone know; members should be non-judgmental and non-critical; etc.: whatever your group decides works best for everyone.

- A typical agenda might be five minutes of social time; a timed go-around the table to briefly share recent successes; a timed go-around to share a particular challenge or problem; open discussion and problem-solving for each member's challenges.

Mastermind groups build their own momentum and energy; it's an interesting dynamic! It can only help your business, as you will probably continue to raise the bar and do better, knowing you've got cheerleaders who are rooting for you and will challenge you if you haven't met your goals.

5. What You Need

Let's discuss what you'll need to start and run your business.

5.1 Equipment

There is some general equipment you should acquire that will make your life as a personal historian easier.

5.1a Computer

Your number one priority is a fast, powerful, reliable computer. You'll be spending a lot of time at it, corresponding with clients, answering queries from potential clients, transcribing, writing, editing, proofreading, importing and editing scans of photographs, laying out your books, and researching. On the administrative side, you'll be archiving clients' files, keeping track of your time, and doing bookkeeping. If you're going to buy a new computer, make sure it has a big enough hard drive and lots of memory. I won't wade in to the PC or Mac debate as you probably already have a favorite between the two.

Do you need a laptop? If you're lucky enough to have a cottage or you travel frequently and you need to do some work while you're away, invest in a laptop. It's essential if you're giving presentations to groups about personal history, or showing a potential client your website or a portfolio of your work. You could also take it to a client's house along with a portable scanner, and upload your scans right then and there.

5.1b Printer

You'll need a printer for a number of reasons: printing invoices for clients, e-receipts, research findings, proof copies, and much more. Unless you're planning to print books yourself — in which case you have a big investment ahead of you — a general workhorse-type printer will give you what you need, quality and speed wise. Color is nice to have but not absolutely necessary. You can get colored letterhead and other business stationery printed at your local print shop or online.

When you're shopping for a printer, you'll have to choose between inkjet or laser. For business purposes (as opposed to printing photographs just for personal use), a laser printer is best. The toner cartridges are more expensive, but they last a lot longer than inkjet cartridges so your long-run operations costs are actually lower. Laser printers are also faster.

Multi-use printers that also function as scanners and copiers (and fax machines; does anyone fax anymore?) not only save space on your desk, but they probably also save money in the long run because you don't need to buy each machine separately. Just make sure the machine you buy is compatible with your computer. I bought a fairly expensive beast of a multi-use printer/scanner/copier, assured by the label and by the salesman that it was completely compatible with my Mac. Not so; I can't use the scanner. I didn't bother returning it because I was under a deadline and I'm happy with the copying and printing functions, and I already had another scanner. But do your due diligence. If you have to stretch the budget to buy high quality equipment that will see you into the future, do so.

More and more machines are going wireless, so if that's important to you, check it out. Look at what's included with your printer, too.

Some don't include a cable, which you might need. That can add $20 or $30 to the bottom line. Most printers can print envelopes and standard paper sizes, but if you plan on printing on heavier stock, say, for a cover of a coil-bound manuscript on a regular basis, do your research. You can always go to your local print shop for the occasional special job.

5.1c Scanner

Scanners are useful for more than just scanning photographs and documents. If you want to email something that is not a Word document, you can scan it as a PDF (portable document file) and then attach it to your email. (If you're using a Mac, you can save something as a PDF by choosing Print, then "Save as PDF.") Again, make sure your scanner will be compatible with your computer, and make sure it has the chops to give you good quality scans.

5.1d Digital recorder: No more cassette tapes

My very first paying personal history project came unexpectedly and caught me unprepared equipment-wise; I had no time to get a new recording device, so I used a beat-up old Radio Shack tape recorder with duct tape holding the battery compartment closed. Apart from what my client must have thought about my highly sophisticated, professional-looking equipment, I cringe when I think of the fragility of the thing and how I relied on it to capture all those precious life stories!

That was in the days before digital recorders, which have revolutionized the personal history field. Some personal historians still use tape recorders, and others use them as back-up in case their digital recorder conks out, but it's getting harder to even find cassette tapes to buy and they will soon be obsolete.

Much like how digital cameras capture images, digital recorders capture sound. The files can be easily transferred to a computer, where they can be reproduced, transferred to other formats, and edited without losing quality. The beauty of digital recording includes the following:

- Recorders are lightweight, small, and easy to use.

- They hold hours of recording that are difficult to erase accidentally.

- Recorders connect directly to your computer and transfer the files quickly. You can then erase the files on the recorder's memory card and record again and again.

- Some recorders have excellent internal microphones so you don't even need an external mic.

- Some recorders have adjustable sound levels.

- The audio files are excellent quality, can be edited to remove long silences or gaffes, can have tracks added to segment the file, are easy to organize, and can be sent over the Internet.

- With software and a foot pedal, the audio files can be transcribed into text files.

Tip: Never rely on batteries, ever (unless you're out in the field — outside, on location — and if you are, take lots of fresh batteries). Plug your recorder into an electrical outlet (bring a power cord in case you need an extension).

Digital recorders are becoming more sophisticated and, like a lot of technological equipment, are actually coming down in price, so shop around. You can spend a lot of money on a digital recorder, but you don't have to — certainly not when you're starting out. You may find that a low-cost or mid-range recorder is just fine for your purposes. You can do a lot of research online, then go to a bricks-and-mortar store. Stores that sell musical instruments and recording equipment are more likely to have knowledgeable salespeople that can help you find the right make and model.

Whatever model of digital recorder you buy, look for the following features:

- able to run on AC power (plugged into a normal electrical outlet) or batteries,

- able to record in stereo using two external microphones; therefore you need a connection for an external microphone (XLR professional audio type),

- a clearly visible control panel that tells you sound level and most importantly, that the "record" function is working,

- able to record in uncompressed WAV (.wav) audio file format at CD quality (16-bit/44.1 kHz),

- a USB connection for uploading sound files to your computer,

- a built-in stereo mic,

- able to record in a readily available, high-capacity storage medium such as an SD (Secure Digital) memory card, and

- an auto-tracking feature that lets you break up the files into a manageable size for burning onto a CD.

5.1e Microphones

You may want to buy external microphones, depending on what you plan to do with your recordings. If you're delivering CDs to a client, microphones will give superior sound quality. You can choose a tabletop, standing, or a lavalier mic (also known as a lapel mic because it clips on to your narrator's clothing), but you may find that the built-in microphone on your recorder is fine. If you do decide to buy an external microphone, research what is best for your purposes and what is compatible with your digital recorder.

5.1f Foot pedal for transcribing

A foot pedal works in conjunction with transcribing software. Much like the old dictaphone pedals, this machine is controlled by your foot (or feet) to play, stop, rewind, advance, or slow the recording that is playing on your computer. Score another point for technology! In the old days of tape recorders, you had to press Play, type like crazy while it was still in your head … *oh wait, did she say "stamp" or "staple"?* Stop the tape, rewind it, play it again. It took forever to get two 45-minute tapes transcribed.

You can use keyboard commands instead of a foot pedal. It's a matter of personal choice. I like keeping my hands free to type like crazy and let my feet control the audio flow. Foot pedals plug into a USB port on your computer.

5.1g Business phone/answering machine/voicemail

When potential customers call your number, what are they going to hear? If your budget allows, get a separate phone line, especially if several people in your house are using the phone. Potential customers may be trying to reach you but can't because the phone is always busy. Rather than leave a message, some will go on to the next business that has a real live person answering the phone. If you're home alone most of the day this shouldn't be a problem as long as you aren't tying up the phone.

A more affordable option is to just make your current message inclusive of your business. "Hello, you've reached the Jones residence and the offices of Jones Memoirs. Please leave a message and we will return your call as soon as possible."

5.1h CDs/DVDs, printer paper, file folders

You might be using a lot of CDs for your recorded interviews and perhaps scanned photographs as well. Keep a good supply on hand. You don't want to have an important deadline looming only to find you have to take an hour to go to the store for supplies. You'll also need all the usual office supplies such as paper, file folders, paper clips, highlighters, pens, etc.

5.1i Digital camera

A camera is useful for taking photos of heirlooms, documents and photos that are too fragile for scanning. Sometimes a photograph of a photograph is as clear as a scan.

5.1j Shredder

Your clients' life stories should be held in strict confidence. You'll have a lot of proof copies, transcripts, notes, etc. relating to your clients' projects, and rather than putting all that paper in the recycling bin, consider buying a shredder. The last thing you want is your clients' private information blowing all over the street!

5.1k External hard drive

An external hard drive, or USB key, comes in very handy if you need to transfer work from one computer to another.

5.2 Software

I'll go over some software that you may want to consider.

5.2a Microsoft Office

Invest in an up-to-date suite of Microsoft Office. You want file formats that are compatible with most other computers; not only Word documents but Excel and PowerPoint as well.

5.2b Adobe Reader

You need Adobe Reader to view PDFs (Portable Document Format files). The good news is it's free. Google "Adobe Reader" to download.

5.2c Photo editing software

Clients will give you photographs of varying degrees of quality and suitability, and may ask that you just crop out the neighbor or otherwise alter the image. Though you could probably make do with the photo-editing software that came with your camera or computer, make your life easier by investing in a program with more muscle. I like Photoshop Elements, a "lite" version of Photoshop.

5.2d Contact management software

There will come a day when you know you're spending way too much time looking for the contact information for a client, contractor, supplier, chamber of commerce, library … and you vow to change your ways. Having a well-organized contact management system is especially important now that everyone's got more than one email address, a Twitter name, Facebook page, cell phone number, home phone number, website … you get the picture. If you're on a Mac, you'll find the Address Book that came with your computer probably has all you need. For Windows Vista users, there's Windows Contacts. You could also look into Microsoft Outlook, or the Web-based Gmail/Google Contacts, Web-based Plaxo, Now X or Now Up-to-Date, and Contact 5. There is a dizzying array of software, and yes, it takes a bit of time to figure out, but your contact database is only going to grow, so it's very wise to get it set up and organized before you get too busy.

5.3 Workspace

To me, the most important piece of a good workspace is a door. I need complete silence when I'm writing or editing. Even the thought of an interruption can break my concentration. Apart from that, here's what I recommend for a first-class workspace in your home:

1. A comfortable chair is crucial. This is one thing you shouldn't skimp on. A good chair with support will last you for a decade or more.

2. A desk that's big enough to hold piles of papers, your computer, an assortment of pens and highlighters, file holders, a printer, a scanner, a telephone, and preferably a large empty spot where you can spread out a manuscript and photos.

3. Containers to hold boxes of photographs and manuscripts and a space to keep them. Since the photographs will be returned to the client and you can destroy the manuscript once the project is finished, these containers don't need any special archival qualities. Some plastic ones of varying sizes will be fine.

4. Recycling bin for all that paper.

5. Bookshelves: As your business grows, you'll collect your favorite books about life stories, memoirs, the personal history business (hopefully this book), family history, photo preservation, etc. You'll also have lots of reference books.

5.4 Reference books and subscriptions

5.4a Books

You'll gradually fill your bookshelves with your favorite "must-haves" — those books you refer to again and again. On my shelves I have dictionaries: *Canadian Oxford* and *Webster's* for both Canadian and American spellings, *Roget's Thesaurus*, *Fowler's Modern English Usage*,

Elements of Style, Associated Press Style Guide and *Canadian Press Style Guide*, and dozens of reference books on life-story writing, historical timelines, and social history. I use the online *Chicago Manual of Style*, which is essential for manuscript preparation.

5.4b Subscriptions

In any business, you need to be up on what's happening in the world and in your community. There are countless leads and opportunities waiting in the pages of your newspapers and magazines. Read an article about a local business celebrating an anniversary? Drop a congratulatory note to the owner along with an offer to write the company history. A magazine article says that the government is giving grants for local history projects? Find out how you can qualify.

Besides subscriptions to printed material (and who doesn't like getting real mail these days?), you can subscribe to online e-zines, news sites, and specialty sites like Ancestry.com or Ancestry.ca. There are countless e-newsletters about marketing, seniors' issues, memoir writing, and writers' resources that offer quick tips and news items.

Worth every penny is an online backup system. I don't think I could sleep at night without the assurance that if the house burns down, my files are safely stored off site and can be retrieved within minutes. I much prefer this method to an external hard drive, which I'd probably lose!

5 PRICING

Pricing is one of the most difficult — and most important — issues in a personal history business. Even personal historians who have completed dozens of projects grapple with how much to charge because of the unique nature of every project. Take time to carefully decide on your pricing strategy; it will save you a lot of grief down the road.

You'll soon discover the personal rewards for doing this work. This chapter will help you determine the financial ones.

1. Pricing Strategy

How will you price your products and services? If you price yourself too low, customers question your ability and the value of your offering. Not only that, you'll eventually throw in the towel because you can make more money flipping burgers. But if you price yourself too high, you risk losing sales. Smart pricing takes research, experience, and business and marketing savvy.

1.1 Good, better, best

One marketing concept surrounding pricing is to offer products at three price points: the good, better, best approach. You cover all your bases: One consumer might want something simple at a low cost, another will buy a beefed-up version priced a little higher, and someone else will opt for the top-of-the-line. As a personal historian you're in a good position to offer a wide variety of products or services at various price points. Capturing the stories and history is the main thing; in a way, all the rest is packaging. If a customer can't afford the deluxe leather hardcover book right now, sell a scaled-down version for a fraction of the price. If the budget for a whole life story project isn't available, suggest a shorter project with a narrower focus — say, his or her trip to Europe, or a family cookbook. You get the idea.

1.2 Your position in the marketplace

Your pricing strategy needs to take into account where you are, both geographically and in the industry marketplace. Factors affecting this include the following:

- **Geographic Location:** Where you live does affect what you can reasonably charge. Most services are more expensive in the affluent neighborhoods of a big city than they are in a small town.

- **High-end niche, or affordable and accessible?:** Are you targeting the high-end market with custom books in the range of $10,000 upward? This kind of project will obviously take up a lot of your time — not only in doing the work, but in finding the few clients willing to spend that much. Or do you plan to try to get lots of clients who want less-expensive products?

- **What is the going rate for similar services?:** Look on personal historians' websites in your general area or in a similar-sized town or location. Be careful when you weigh this factor, because you don't know how successful those businesses are. Just because they charge $100 per hour doesn't mean they're getting much business. Try to find standard rates for researchers, genealogists, writers, and editors. Check individuals',

companies', and associations' websites, which usually have some guidelines.

- **Experience and reputation:** Starting out, you may want to set a lower rate as you learn the ropes. If you're charging a premium price, you'll want to be able to back it up with some samples and demonstrated expertise.

1.3 Other factors determining your pricing strategy

1.3a Cost and value

Pricing involves cost and value. Cost is how much you have to spend to produce something — that is, your labor and the cost of materials. Value is the benefit to the consumer. As much as possible, think about not only what it costs you, but what its perceived worth is to your customer. Remember that when it comes to products that are close to the heart and which answer an emotional need, price becomes less of a factor in the buying decision. What is it worth to your customers to capture the firsthand accounts of a loved one and preserve them forever as a family legacy? If you can convey that worth, your products will almost sell themselves.

1.3b Prices can be fluid

You also have to discover what the customer is willing to pay. You'll quickly find out your prices are too high if customer after customer seems initially interested — the light seems to be green for go — but people back out on hearing how much it's going to cost. You'll also discover, if you keep good records, if you're pricing yourself too low. Regularly review your strategy — how you price your products and your position in the market *vis-à-vis* your competition.

1.3c Compensating for special circumstances

Think of different scenarios, long term, and of the broad spectrum of your customer base, too. Will you offer a lower price to people who just can't afford to spend much money but you'd really like to help? Will you be doing volunteer or *pro bono* work? Will you offer a discount for repeat customers or multiple projects? Pay for referrals? Will you have a loss-leader (a low-priced offering designed to hook a customer and entice him or her into buying a higher-priced product)? Will you negotiate your prices? Offer specials for certain holidays such as Father's Day? You don't necessarily have to have a written policy for all these situations, but they are something to keep in mind when you determine your prices.

2. Methodology: Hourly Charge or Package Price?

Are you going to offer a package price, or charge by the hour? Here are some considerations.

2.1 Hourly charge pros and cons

On the plus side, charging hourly means that you could have a regular cash flow. It's also reasonably simple: You work and then get paid for the number of hours you worked. Plus, you get paid fairly and your client only pays for actual work done. Many personal historians choose this method for those reasons. However, you should consider these possible downsides:

- There's more paperwork involved with invoices and receipts.

- You could find yourself waiting for payment and be in the unappealing position of having to send reminders to your customer.

- You have to reveal your hourly rate. Some people will balk at what they consider a high rate (if that's what you're charging). Set a rate that you've determined you need to cover your overhead and the normal costs of running a business. Steer clear of customers who question you on it. If you've decided that you need to charge $75 per hour in order to make your business viable and sustainable, stick with it. You're not a subcontractor or an employee, in which case your hourly rate doing what you do would probably be lower. But you are in business and your costs are higher. Think about what other professionals charge per hour, such as your plumber, hairstylist, massage therapist, appliance repair person, or personal trainer. Don't underrate what you're worth.

- It's open-ended. Customers won't know what the final tally will be, which is a scary thing for some people. If you do charge by the hour, give people an estimate of how long you think it's going to take to complete the project. Explain the process and don't sugarcoat. Tell them all the things you'll be charging for; tell them all the extra tasks that go into a project, like preparing questions, doing research, two or more rounds of proofreading, etc.

Whether you charge by the hour or by a package price, keep careful track of every minute you spend on a project, within reason. If I spend 10 or 15 minutes I'll usually jot it down, but not less than that. You'll be amazed at how the time adds up. I staple a time-tracking form to the inside of each client's folder and jot down when I worked, for how long, and what the task was. See Sample 9 for an example of a time tracking form.

TIME TRACKING FORM

Date	Task	Time Spent	Category
August 4, 2010	Interview at McAllister home	2.5 hours	Interviewing
August 4, 2010	Travel to and from interview	1.5 hours	Travel
August 6, 2010	Transcribe audio file from August 4 interview	5 hours	Transcribing
August 8, 2010	Finish transcribing audio from August 4 interview	2 hours	Transcribing
August 10, 2010	Edit August 4 transcript	3 hours	Editorial
August 15	Continue editing August 4 transcript	4.25 hours	Editorial
August 16	Research at county archives	1.5 hours	Research
August 25	Contact designers for quote	45 minutes	Design/ Sub-contracting

2.1a Hourly charge terms of payment

Decide how often you'll invoice your client. State your terms in your contract or letter of agreement.

Ask for a healthy deposit up front — perhaps a quarter of what you anticipate the total fee will be. State that this initial payment represents "the first ten hours of work" or whatever it amounts to. Once you've earned the amount of the initial payment, give your client a statement of how you earned out that advance (an advance earn-out statement). Unless he or she demands it, you don't have to itemize every single task, but from your time tracking form you'll know how much you spent on transcribing, administrative tasks, editing, etc., so you can give him or her a detailed breakdown.

2.2 Package price pros and cons

After doing a couple of projects and carefully tracking your time, you'll learn how many hours it takes to complete a typical personal history, so you might choose to make it simple and quote a price that includes everything from start to finish.

Remember when the all-inclusive vacation gained popularity? What a concept! No fiddling with cash on the beach! Bring me another "free" margarita! There's something very appealing about the all-inclusive — certainly for the consumer, and for you too. The price is agreed upon right up front and money need not enter the conversation again.

The main advantage to the package price is that it's a nice tidy sum. The client knows exactly what it's going to cost, and you have a commitment for a (hopefully) lucrative job.

One disadvantage is that the client can get sticker shock on hearing a package price, which, for a complete life story in a hardcover book with photographs, can be anywhere from $3,000 to $30,000 and upward.

If people do reel at the price it could be partially because they don't understand the extent of the work that goes into creating a personal history, and that's where you come in. You need to explain all the steps involved, how much time each takes, and all the variables that affect costs. You need to believe that the price is worth it — and you'll know that it is because you remember the hundreds of hours that went into your last project!

A disadvantage is that it's very hard to predict exactly how much time it will take. More about this in section **3**.

Tip: When asked how much a personal history costs, you might want to use this analogy: A personal history costs about the same as a vacation. It just depends whether you want a camping trip in the Rockies or a world cruise on a luxury liner.

3. Pricing Your Services for Profit

3.1 Determining project scope: How much does a typical personal history cost?

There are no quick and easy answers when you're asked to determine a price for a personal history project. These are some of the things that will determine your costs:

- Number of interviews required: Fewer interviews obviously take less real time to do. However, another important factor is that the fewer the interviews there are, the less editing time is required for the whole project.

- Number of people being interviewed.

- The interviews themselves: Does the story-teller tell his or her stories in a beginning-to-end fashion, or in fragments that need to be sewn together? Will a light edit suffice, or do you need a massive reorganization? Will you need to do a lot of research to give the stories context? Will your transcriber have difficulty understanding a thick accent? All of these things are almost impossible to predict ahead of time.

- Travel time.

- Is it a whole life story or just one event or period, such as about a military career or surviving a traumatic event or illness? Is it a family history spanning generations?

- The desired end product: Is it an oral history on CD? Straight transcript? Lightly edited transcript? A fully edited manuscript? Book with photographs?

For a life or family history published in a book, it's wise to quote and work in phases. Phase 1 is the preparation of the manuscript, and Phase 2 is book publication. This is because it is impossible to give an accurate price to design and publish a book until you know a) how long the text will be; b) how many photographs and how much touch-up or even restoration will be required; c) what kind of printing and binding the customer wants; and d) his or her choice of paper, cover, quantity, and more. It's much easier to estimate how long it will take to prepare a manuscript. There are still many variables, but it's possible, with experience, to fairly accurately estimate how long it will take you.

3.2 Phase 1: The manuscript

Creating a life story manuscript takes a lot of time. The actual interview time spent with the client accounts for perhaps only 10 percent of the total time you need from start to finish. Here's what you'll be doing on a typical project:

ADVANCE EARN-OUT STATEMENT

Dear Mrs. Jones,

This is the first of a regular update on the status of your family history project. As you know, we've had four interviews of two hours each, on [dates], and I've been transcribing and editing as I go. I've now reached the number of hours covered by the initial retainer of $ _____.

Below is a general breakdown of my time.

Interviewing: 8 hours

Transcribing: 32 hours

Editing: 10 hours

In total, I have worked 50 hours as of today, _____ [date]. As we continue our interviews with your relatives, I will be keeping track of my hours and will send you a new invoice at the beginning of each month.

I'm enjoying working with you. See you next Monday at 2:00 p.m.

Sincerely,

[Name]

- Consulting with the client about the scope and goals; scheduling interviews

- Preliminary research and information gathering

- Traveling to the client's home for interviews

- Setting up recording equipment

- Interviewing

- Transcribing, editing, writing, additional research, making client's changes, copy-editing, proofreading

Watch for hidden demands on your time. On top of the tasks outlined above, you'll spend time on an initial inquiry from your client, preparing a proposal, reviewing the proposal with the client, drawing up a contract, reviewing the contract, setting up your files, trips to the post office, securing permissions, burning CDs, phone calls and correspondence to the client and to subcontractors, and many other little things.

Every project is unique, and every personal historian will work at different speeds and levels of efficiency, but there is one popular formula for calculating how long it will take to create a manuscript in a typical personal history project of about ten hours of interviews. Here it is.

For each hour of recorded interview, it can require anywhere from 15 to 20 hours to prepare a publishable manuscript. By "publishable" I mean transcribed, edited, organized, rewritten where necessary, copyedited, proofread, revised with narrator's changes, proofread again, formatted with chapter breaks and titles, and front matter such as dedications, title page, and copyright page (if applicable), all letter perfect and ready to go. If you're also writing photo captions and doing a lot of research you'd probably be at the upper end of that 20 hours.

Let's say a client hears about you and calls you up, asking how much it would cost to do her father's life story. Once you determine the scope of the project (see above), you can propose a certain number of hours of interviews. In my experience, it's difficult to tell a whole life story in less than 6 hours of interviews. Ideally it's good to allow 10 to 12 hours.

Using the formula, for 8 hours of interviews, it could take you another 120 to 160 hours to complete the manucript. For 10 hours of interviews, it could take you another 150 to 200 hours to complete the manuscript. So in order to price it for your client, you simply multiply that by your hourly rate. Here are a few scenarios:

8 hours of interviews =
128 hours of work x $75/hour = $9,600

8 hours of interviews =
128 hours of work x $50/hour = $6,400

8 hours of interviews =
128 hours of work x $40/hour = $5,120

8 hours of interviews =
168 hours of work x $75/hour = $12,600

8 hours of interviews =
168 hours of work x $50/hour = $8,400

8 hours of interviews =
168 hours of work x $40/hour = $6,720

10 hours of interviews =
160 hours of work x $75/hour = $12,000

10 hours of interviews =
160 hours of work x $50/hour = $8,000

10 hours of interviews =
160 hours of work x $40/hour = $6,400

10 hours of interviews =
210 hours of work x $75/hour = $15,750

10 hours of interviews =
210 hours of work x $50/hour = $10,500

10 hours of interviews =
210 hours of work x $40/hour = $8,400

As you can see, the costs can vary widely. The biggest factor, apart from your hourly rate, is how long it takes you to edit and organize the material you get from the transcripts — and you won't really know that for sure until you start. (Transcribing is more straightforward. A standard rate is 3.5 to 5 hours of transcribing time per hour of audio.) The more interview hours, the more material you'll have to work with, so it's naturally going to take more time to edit and organize the material. It also depends on how your narrator talks. Some people are eloquent and tell a story beginning to end in one go; others jump all over the place and it takes three interview sessions to tell the whole story. They may mix up their facts, which requires you to double-check and do some research. You will constantly be making judgment calls about choice of words, organization, whether something fits better elsewhere or doesn't fit at all, and dozens of other decisions.

3.2a Setting an hourly rate

What do you need to charge per hour? $25? $100? One way to determine your hourly rate is to decide how much annual income you want to make from your business, including profit, expenses, and overhead. Then, divide that number by the number of billable hours — the number of hours you will actually be paid for — that you expect to work in the year. Don't forget to take into account all the time you'll spend on marketing, office maintenance, sourcing suppliers, finding subcontractors, sick days, vacation, etc. Be realistic.

For example, say you want to make $40,000 per year. If your expenses and overhead (and taxes) are $10,000, you need to get paid $50,000. If you expect that you'll be working on paid projects for 20 hours a week (these are the hours for which you will be able to bill a client), and you'll actually only work for 48 weeks out of the 52 weeks in a year (allowing for vacation and other time off), that means you'll be working for 960 hours in the year. Divide $50,000 by 960 and you get $52.08 for your hourly rate.

3.2b Your quote: Estimated range or fixed?

You might want to quote the client an estimated price range. For instance, "I anticipate that the total cost will be in the range of $3,000 to $4,000." Explain that you will keep careful track of your time and only charge for the actual hours worked. This way there won't be any nasty surprises for your client and indeed, if you can do it in less time, you gain several goodwill points for coming in under budget. You'll be protected, too, and get paid fairly for your work. What you don't want to do is go above your highest estimate, unless there are many extenuating circumstances. And if they arise, be sure to talk to your client and warn that the price might creep up higher than you originally planned.

The alternative is to set a firm package price, knowing that for some projects it will take you more time and you'll be working for a lower rate than you want, and for other projects it will take you less time and you'll come out ahead. A package price might include, for instance, up to ten hours of interviews, or you could charge a certain amount for each hour of interviewing, knowing what each hour of interviewing amounts to in "back-end" time on your part.

My advice is to do several projects before setting a package price, until you have a very accurate measure of how many hours go into a typical project. Then you just have to assess whether each new project is indeed a typical one! Is ten hours with Mr. Jones going to take you the same amount of time as ten hours with Mrs. Smith?

You can see why pricing a personal history manuscript can be a challenge!

3.3 Phase 2: Book publication
3.3a What to charge

Once you have a completed manuscript and you know how many photos will be included, you can figure out what it's going to cost to publish the book. This phase is a little simpler to quote on, if you are outsourcing the design work. Then, it's just a matter of getting a quote from a designer, printer, and bookbinder and adding your own markup (10–15 percent or more). Get at least three quotes from different subcontractors, making sure you're giving them exactly the same specifications and responsibilities.

You'll also want to charge for your time for managing the production flow, which includes getting quotes from suppliers, consulting with the client, consulting with the designer, doing the paperwork and other administrative tasks, proofreading, and delivery.

Even if you're hiring a designer, you'll have many tasks to perform, for which you may want to charge an hourly fee. If you have a good scanner you can scan photos yourself; charge an hourly fee, or a "per image" fee.

If you do the book layout yourself, I recommend you charge by the hour and give your closest estimate of the final price — again, a range is best. Because there are so many factors involved, there is also a bulk of information that will help you decide how to price book production in Chapters 6 and 7.

3.3b Hidden demands on your time and money

Be aware of all that you do for a client. It's easy to forget about the little things that eat up your time and cost you money. Some of these include:

- Organizing photos and documents; identifying them physically by writing on the back of them or attaching sticky notes, and electronically on your computer

- Researching copyright material and getting permissions

- Long-distance and local phone calls

- Emails

- Preparing frontmatter such as an introduction and dedication

3.3c Extras for income: Would you like fries with that?

Think of add-ons that you could offer your client, such as:

- Working with a genealogist (or doing it yourself) to research the family's roots

- Creating a diagram of a family tree

- Creating a map of the narrator's childhood neighborhood, town, county, etc.

- Touching-up or restoring old photos

3.3d Project creep and how to avoid it

Beware of how a project's agreed-upon parameters can balloon and inevitably cost you more time.

- "I found a few more photos that would be great in Chapter 3." **How it costs you:** For every photograph, there's extra time scanning, editing, and writing captions.

- "Aunt Ethel has some diaries from 1932. Could you just look them over and see if we should include them?" **How it costs you:** As well as reading the diaries, you'd have to examine how they'd fit into the book, consult with the client, etc.

- "Grant thinks we should take out the part about his father going bankrupt." **How it costs you:** It's never a case of simply deleting something. You might possibly have to rearrange a good chunk of text, remove any references, etc. And, you've already transcribed and edited the part about Grant's father.

Project creep is when a project starts involving more work on your part without the budgeted money to back it up. It's vital that your contract spells out exactly what is included in your fee. It's especially important at the review stage. This is when the client will see everything written down and realize he or she forgot to include something or that the baby picture he or she previously told you was Uncle Joe is in fact Uncle Bob and he or she wants to replace it. Not only have you scanned, formatted, and written the caption for the mistaken photo, you now have to do it again for the real one. Stipulate up front how many hours you will spend on the revision to the first draft ("not to exceed 4 hours" or whatever you choose).

3.3e Do what you do best and farm out the rest

Decide what you can do most efficiently, and recognize when it's better to outsource and hire some help. For instance, if you can hire a transcriber for less than your own hourly rate, do it — as long as you're not spending just as much time getting the file to him or her, proofreading, or correcting the work. In that case you may as well do it yourself.

If your business is going to grow to the point where you have several clients at any given time, you can't possibly handle everything yourself. Sure you could do everything yourself — and burn out. Maybe not at the beginning (and of course you may want to remain a one-person operation), but you will probably eventually need the services of a writer, editor, proofreader, graphic designer or layout artist, photographer, researcher, or genealogist. Try to determine if you'll be needing outside help before you quote on a project, because you'll have to take into account those subcontractors' fees as well as what you'll be tacking on as a mark-up and include that in your quote. If you haven't allowed for outside help and you're in the middle of a project and have to hire somebody, chances are you'll only break even on that part of the project. But at least you'll get the project done and keep your client happy.

3.3f Should you discount your prices?

What should you do when a client asks for a discount? Don't be pressured into thinking you need to give an answer right then and there, but it's a good idea to have some basic policies in place.

Whether to give a discount is a personal choice, of course; you decide what's right for you. I do not recommend it, but there are a few instances when I think a discount could be appropriate.

- The client could lead to more work; either another project with them, or their family, or one of their connections.

- He or she simply can't spend that much money. This is a tough call, but you have to go with your gut sometimes.

- It's a project you believe in and one that would give you a great deal of personal satisfaction.

- It's a prestigious, high-profile project that will help get your name known.

- The client agrees to pay you a greater portion of your normal up-front fees.

- The client provides you with a discount on something he or she sells.

- You need the work and you decide it's better to lower your rate than not work at all.

6
PRODUCE A SAMPLE

It's time to get started on a real project and produce a sample. This step in your business is vitally important, for four very good reasons:

1. You'll have something tangible to show potential customers.

2. You need to do the work in order to understand it.

3. You can decide if you like the work, and determine in which areas you're strongest and in which areas you need help.

4. It will help you determine what you need to charge.

1. Produce a Sample for Your Customers

Most people will have trouble envisioning a privately-published memoir or family history book. Some people can't believe that a book published privately is as good as something produced by a "real" publisher. Seeing is believing. Also, some people don't understand the difference between first-person and third-person narrative. When they read an excerpt such as, "When I discovered I was going to have twins, life changed," they get a better sense of the fact that you publish firsthand accounts based on interviews. They can also see how others have told their stories. It starts them thinking about what to include in their own story. They can start to imagine their lives in chapters, as a whole story, and see how photographs can be used to enhance the story. And they see that their words — their memories, anecdotes, thoughts, and feelings — can be preserved forever. Nothing else in your marketing toolkit will be as powerful as a sample.

Showing a sample also allows you to talk about the amount of work involved. Take along the raw transcript so potential clients can see how you transformed those long, rambling, disjointed pages into neat, well-written chapters.

Make your sample as impressive and professional-looking as you possibly can, inside and out, and be ready to speak knowledgeably about what's involved in getting from this initial conversation to the moment your client can hold the book in his or her hands. It will cost you some money to produce a handsome book (or other product), but it will be worth it.

Potential clients will probably ask the cost of the book they're holding, so be ready to answer those questions. Explain that this is just a sample and there are lots of options and different choices depending on the length of interviews, number of photographs, type of book, etc.

If you don't plan to publish books, do a sample of whatever product you plan to focus on, whether it's a memory quilt, photo montage, wall hanging, or an oral history CD.

2. Produce a Sample for Yourself

What you learn from doing this will give your work authenticity and help you realize the emotional value of it. Confucius said: "What I hear, I forget. What I see, I remember. What I do, I understand." Do a personal history project that's close to your heart, and you'll understand what you're offering to clients. The subject could be your mother, father, grandfather, grandmother, neighbor, or friend. Ask if family members would like to contribute to the cost. If they don't want to pay up front, you can sell them a book when you're finished. This will help you recoup some

money! Working for someone close to you makes doing it free of charge a little easier to swallow. Ideally, you should also do a book about someone other than your immediate family, because you want to gain experience interviewing people you don't know very well. Find a "good" subject — perhaps someone you know who has some interesting stories about his or her life — and approach this person with the offer to interview him or her and record some stories, then put those stories into a book.

3. Produce a Sample for Your Pricing Plans

Do a sample that's similar to what you plan to sell. This is the best way to come up with a pricing structure that makes good business sense. After you're finished you'll know how much time and money it cost you to do a typical project, and you can price similar products based on your findings.

3.1 Time yourself

Producing your sample is like going to Personal History University. You will learn so much, every step of the way. Research as much as possible before every phase. Get quotes, make notes, even keep a personal diary about your first personal history project! Keep careful track of every task and how long you spend on it, plus any challenges you meet along the way, a list of resources, and what you'd do differently next time. See Sample 11 for a sample time tracker. A blank form is also available on the CD-ROM included with this book.

When you're finished, you'll know what goes into a project, you'll know exactly how long it took you to do it (with tasks broken down so you can apply your experience to other projects), and how much it cost. You'll also have a sample you'll be proud to display as the first in your portfolio, and you'll have given someone a priceless gift.

TIME TRACKER FOR SAMPLE PERSONAL HISTORY

Name of Project: _____

Name of Subject/Narrator: _____

Start Date: _____

Task	Time It Took	Problems	Lesson Learned
Interview	3 hours	Battery failed	Check equipment!
Interview	5 hours	Client was sick	Confirm before going
Talked to client about photos	1 hour	Didn't know how much to charge for scanning	Do test scans/pricing
Transcription	10 hours	Couldn't understand him when he talked softly	Mic closer to subject
Editing	25 hours		
Writing captions	8 hours		

3.2 Accounting for expenses

Be sure to write down the cost of every item you buy on behalf of this sample, from paper to batteries, to CDs, printing, and binding.

4. Free or Not?

Whether to charge the subject of your project is tricky and entirely a personal choice. On the one hand, you're using this person as your "guinea pig" and this is your learning curve, so why should he or she pay you? On the other hand, you could end up working at least a hundred hours, and it sure would be nice to get some compensation. In addition, the subject is receiving something of great value. You could suggest that you'd like to do this project at a greatly discounted rate in return for the subject understanding it's your first project and forgiving mistakes — and giving you a client testimonial you can quote in your marketing material.

Even if you do the whole sample free of charge, the experience you'll get is worth it. Another plus: not charging means a little less pressure. You can take your time and work by trial and error, which is the best way to learn anything, right?

Be sure you get permission from the narrator of your sample book to show it as part of your portfolio. Make this a stipulation when you choose a subject for your sample.

5. Help! I Don't Have a Sample But I Do Have a Lead!

You may not have finished your first sample personal history project when you have the opportunity to meet with a potential client — one who's going to pay you! Don't panic. I fretted about this too, wondering how I could explain that I hadn't actually had a client yet. I did have some writing samples, and did a lot of research so it sounded like I knew what I was talking about! I went to the bookstore and invested in a couple of books that looked like what I wanted to produce for clients. But I never had to show them to anyone; my first few clients didn't ask to see a sample. Neither did they ask for references. (Since then I've been asked for both.) So don't let not having something to show stop you from giving your best sales pitch. If you can, put together a binder with a sample of your writing, a one-page description of your services, a short biography, and anything else that shows you're a professional.

You could also just 'fess up and say, "You'll be my first personal history client." Then explain what experience you bring to your new business (show a writing sample if you have it), and why you are doing it — demonstrating your passion and knowledge of the field. If the potential client asks why he or she should take a chance on hiring someone with no direct experience, you could say something like, "Because I am determined to make this business successful. As my first client, you can know that I'm going to give everything I can to your project and make sure you're a satisfied customer. My future might depend on it, so you have my guarantee that no one will work as hard as I will."

Could he or she really say no?

Tip: A word of caution. Never lend your sample books out unless you know the person very well. Remember all the hard work and money that went into the sample and guard it accordingly!

6. Steps to Create a Personal History (Sample or Paid Project)

Here are the basic steps you'll follow when creating a personal history. Chapter 7 delves into more detail on the steps required when doing your first paid project.

1. Do an introductory pre-interview with the narrator, either in person or by phone, to discuss the scope of the project and topics for interviews.

2. Get the client to sign a contract and agree on a pricing scheme (see Samples 4 and 5 in Chapter 4).

3. Set up a rough interview schedule.

4. Do background research to familiarize yourself with the narrator's hometown, occupation, experiences, etc.

5. Prepare a list of questions for interviews.

6. Conduct and record interviews with the narrator and any other contributors.

7. Transcribe audio recordings. Review transcript before the next interview, if possible.

8. Complete scheduled interviews and begin writing and editing of manuscript.

9. Complete the first draft and send it to the client for revisions.

10. Incorporate revisions, copyedit, proofread (or have your contracted editor do so), and return the final draft to the client.

11. Get sign-off from the client (as seen in Sample 8 in Chapter 4).

12. Select photos, scan, and write captions.

13. Lay out the book or have the designer do so.

14. Send the finalized book to the printer or bookbinder you have chosen.

7
FROM "TESTING, TESTING" TO PRINT: A STEP-BY-STEP GUIDE TO PRODUCING A PERSONAL HISTORY

All right! You're about to start a new personal history project. This is where we get down to the nuts and bolts.

1. Prepare a Project Plan

First things first: Plan. Here's what a project plan should include:

1. Definition of the project. Is it a life story, church history, or family reunion album? Give it a working name.

2. State the goal of the project.

3. Do a schedule. Make a rough timeline, and state who is involved, and where the bulk of the interviews or work will take place.

4. List all the tasks and proposed deadlines as well as time needed to complete the tasks.

5. If you know you'll be using outside help, name the parties involved.

A project plan schedule should take into account your other projects, so consult your calendar before setting deadlines. Involve your client. Talk to him or her about your plans and proposed deadlines. (Besides "How much will it cost?," the question asked most often is "How long will it take?") Consider giving your client a modified project plan that outlines what he or she needs to do to help move the project forward. List the milestones, including understandings, expectations, and processes. An excerpt of one, mid-project, might look something like this:

> Week 6: Interviews Complete. I will send you an invoice for the agreed-upon payment of _____.

> Week 8: I am away on vacation for one week.

> Weeks 9 to 12: The transcribing will be finished and I'll be editing the text to put your stories together, correct grammar, check facts and spelling, and breaking it into paragraphs and chapters.

> Week 12: I will deliver the first draft of the manuscript to you.

> Week 14: You will return the first draft with your changes.

2. The Pre-Interview

You've probably already met with your client — the one who's paying the bill and signing the contract. But the narrator may be the client's parent or grandparent.

Meeting the narrator before you start interviewing him or her can put everyone at ease. You can break the ice with some small talk, get to know each other, and you can explain the process. Most people will have no idea what you're going to do with them, what equipment you use, and how the whole thing works. Without your recorder going, you can have a relaxed conversation. You'll be able to assess the narrator's voice (level, clarity, and accent), scout out the home for a good location to conduct the interview, identify any challenges such as whether your narrator is in a wheelchair or bed, determine where to plug in your recorder, and get a bit of background about them. But don't let them start telling you stories quite yet; advise them before you arrive that this brief (25 minutes or so) meeting is just for introductions and a bit of information gathering. Getting that stuff out of the way before your first interview is a good idea.

However, another school of thought is that you should have the recorder running at the very first meeting (assuming you have an agreement and you'll get paid) because this is often when the narrator says why he's doing this personal history, or sums up his life, makes general statements, etc., and this can be is a good chance to capture that kind of overview.

Tip: If your narrator lives more than an hour away, you might want to do a telephone pre-interview instead of meeting him or her in person.

3. Scheduling the Interviews

3.1 How many interviews do you need?

For an entire life story, try to get a commitment of at least 6 or 7 hours of interviews. Even after 12 hours, I've never had a narrator say, "Well, that's it! That's my whole life story; can't think of anything else," though presumably that would happen at some point! How many interviews you conduct is often dictated by the client's budget and by the scope of the project. A large family history with several narrators will need a lot more interview hours than a single life story.

3.2 How long should you allow for each interview?

Another benefit of a pre-interview is that it allows you to gauge the narrator's mental and physical strength, which greatly affects how long each interview should be. You can also talk to the adult children about this, if they are the paying clients.

In general, a two-hour time frame is long enough, particularly if the narrator is very elderly. Interviewing is an intense process for both you and the narrator, and can be very tiring and draining. Assure your narrator that whatever you schedule, you can usually accommodate changes.

3.3 What's the best time?

Some people feel they have to accommodate your schedule, and will be reluctant to specify a certain time of day or admit to being sleepy right after lunch. Assure them they are your priority and you're available any time — within reason, of course, and taking into consideration all those other clients who are waiting for your visit!

Start immediately. The family will be excited about the project and raring to go, so don't lose momentum. Try to start within a week of the contract signing (and NOT BEFORE you have a contract and deposit). Life is unpredictable. Especially when the narrator is very elderly, anything can happen. Get the stories recorded as soon as you can.

Read more about the interview process in Chapter 8.

4. Transcribing

Transcribing is the process of listening to the audio recording and typing out what is said. I recommend you do your own transcribing when you're starting out, for the following reasons:

- You'll review the interview and get more deeply into the content. You'll notice where the narrator got distracted or veered off on a tangent. Make a note and be sure to revisit that forgotten topic at a future interview.

- You'll notice things about your interviewing technique you'll want to correct in

future. Are you keeping your questions short? Are you asking one question at a time? Are you allowing your narrator to take as much time as needed to answer a question? The stuff that follows what seems to be a long silence (and they are never as long as you think they are) is usually a deeply-felt thought or revelation. Silences are just as important as words, sometimes. (Hint: If your narrator nods off, it's okay to break the silence!)

- You'll appreciate what goes into transcribing and won't balk at a transcriber's invoice or timeframe should you decide to hire one in future.

You can do some simple editing while you're transcribing.

There are rewards, but transcribing is time-consuming (count on about four hours per one hour of audio recording) and can be tedious. You have to listen intently and catch everything. Sometimes you have to play back something three times just to understand what's being said.

You'll need transcribing software. There is free or reasonably-priced software for both Mac and PC, such as ExpressScribe. It's possible to use the software with keystrokes on your keypad, but I prefer a foot pedal. Both methods allow you to play the recording at a comfortable speed, stop, replay, or speed up. You can use headphones or the speakers on your computer; headphones are strongly recommended.

4.1 Hiring a transcriber

There will probably come a time when you want to hire someone to do your transcribing, or at least some of it. You can spend the time you're saving doing more profitable activities, like finding new clients.

4.1a Things to consider when hiring transcribers

- **Confidentiality:** Are they willing to sign a confidentiality agreement? You need to have complete trust that the transcriber will keep the clients' stories in strict confidence.

- **Speed:** Time is money. The faster they can transcribe the less it costs you. However, if the transcript is full of mistakes that you have to correct, you're hardly saving any money, which is why the next point is important.

- **Accuracy:** The best transcribers know enough about history, culture, geography, etc., that they can recognize names, places, events, etc., and spell them correctly, and if they don't know how to spell something, they are smart enough to do some research.

- **Over-the-top good:** The absolute best transcribers will themselves notice and identify where the narrator has his or her facts mixed up. They won't correct them, but they'll alert you so you can correct them (or at least tell your narrator about them; more on this in Chapter 8).

- **Price:** A large transcribing company will probably cost more than an individual. The downside may be that a single person is only one person with 24 hours in the day, so you may find yourself waiting to have your jobs done. When comparing prices, ask how the transcriber charges: by the page, line, or hour?

- **Consistency:** When you use an individual as opposed to a large company, you know exactly who's working on your stuff — the same person who'll get to know your requirements and preferences about style, and who'll get familiar with your narrator's stories, making it easier for him or her to recognize speech patterns, places, and names.

- **Ease of use:** Most transcribers are now using digital equipment, but not all of them are up-to-speed on receiving audio files over the Internet. Some have their own FTP service so you can simply upload your files to their website. We've come a long way from the days when you had to mail your precious audiotapes and hope for the best!

4.2 Style guide

You should give your transcriber a set of guidelines and preferences. These should cover the following:

1. How you want the document formatted. Double-spaced? What font size? Date and client's name at the top?

2. How you want him or her to indicate where he or she can't understand something. Digital audio files show a time marker, which helps immeasurably to find the confusing bit.

3. How you want him or her to distinguish between speakers — different font styles? Full names or initials?

4. How you want him or her to handle phones ringing and subsequent unrelated chitchat. If it's not part of your interview, do you still want it included?

5. Do you want him or her to indicate non-spoken sounds, such as laughter and crying?

6. Your choice of spelling (which dictionary do you want your transcriber to use?) and style (such as how to spell out time

of day: 4 o'clock; 4 p.m.; 4PM, etc.). Even though you'll be editing the transcripts, you can save yourself a little time by having it done right the first time.

7. Do you want the manuscript absolutely strictly verbatim — word for word — with all the "um"s, "er"s, false starts ("So I go — no, wait — in 1982 I went … ")

In general, treat your transcriber like you'd treat any other businessperson. Make an initial inquiry about his or her upcoming schedule, respect his or her time and don't make unreasonable requests, like you "need it yesterday." If possible, give him or her a heads-up a month or so in advance that you have a big project coming up. Pay promptly. Some transcribers use PayPal, which is about as simple a process as you can get.

4.3 Reviewing the transcript

Once the transcript is returned to you, it's good practice to read it while listening to the recording. Even the best transcribers miss things or mess up a phrase here or there, and having been there at the interview you can usually remember the correct word. This review step gives you a chance to make a good clean transcript to work from, plus it immerses you again in the narrator's story. Make notes about what areas warrant revisiting. It will be time well spent.

5. Transcript to Manuscript

5.1 The unique nature of a personal history manuscript

When talking about taking the words from transcript to manuscript, I'll use the word "editing" for the sake of simplicity, but when you're working on a manuscript you'll go much further than what is normally considered editing.

A good personal history manuscript is a skillful blend of original writing and the narrator's own words. It needs a creative hand and demands good writing skills, but also adherence to the narrator's voice. You'll be walking a fine line, constantly making decisions about what to leave in, what to delete, and what to change. You know that a different word or an addition or deletion would make the story more powerful, but you want to stay as close as possible to the original.

A good interview will have yielded a powerful personal account, so hopefully you have a good amount of material with which to work. Some narrators tell their stories eloquently and passionately, with a beginning, middle, and end. But most don't. Most tell a bit here, a bit there, and remember a bit more later on. It's the editor's job to bring all this together.

5.2 First person or third person?

In most cases, a personal history is a first-person account, using the narrator's own words. But if the subject of the personal history is not alive, obviously it will have to be in third person. If this is the case, you have to do a lot more research and the manuscript will require a great deal more of your own writing, using extensive quotes from the people you're interviewing and other sources. You will have consulted with your client before the interviews started as to what exactly you're providing.

In a personal history of a deceased man, I interviewed his daughter and wife and wove their accounts into a third-person narrative, putting his life into historical context from research. Fortunately, the man had kept impeccable records and documents, and the family had hundreds of photos.

Most often, though, the personal histories I do are first-person accounts. The manuscript is told entirely from the point of view of the storyteller, which gives the story immediacy, authenticity, emotion, and power. See Sample 12 for an example of a verbatim transcript and an edited manuscript.

5.3 The editing process

Here's a list of what you will typically do with a raw transcript to turn it into a readable manuscript:

- Make a copy of the raw transcript and save it, untouched. Only make changes to your working copy.

- Read through each transcript.

- Think about structure. Will you tell the story chronologically or by theme? You may have discussed this already with your client. If you decide to change course, be sure you let your client know. (I've found most clients don't care about being involved with this level of the writing process, but it's professional courtesy to keep them apprised of your progress.)

- Create a rough outline based on what you know about the narrator and his or her life.

- Start at the beginning and do your first edit on the material.

- Remove your questions and incorporate them into the narrative so the answer makes sense. For instance:

  Interviewer: You mentioned you were a waitress. Where did you work?

  Narrator: The café down by the tracks.

In the manuscript, you would take out your question so it would read (not part of example):

"I worked as a waitress at the café down by the tracks."

- Delete unnecessary words, repetitions, gibberish, false starts ("So next I went — No wait, it wasn't in '49 — Wait, yes it was — ")

- Note any inconsistencies in the manuscript, and questionable facts. Also note possibly offensive or even libelous material such as hurtful comments, accusations, etc.

- Note where additional research or clarification is required, such as missing dates, unknown places, anecdotes that don't make sense, and so on.

- Make complete sentences by writing them yourself or consolidating two fragments.

- Re-work stories to improve the flow (beginning, middle, end).

- Note places you want to make substantial changes. You can decide later whether to run this by your client or not.

- Insert quotation marks whenever dialogue is included in narrators' stories.

- Make spelling consistent.

- Create a style sheet for each project; a list with place names, people, names of institutions, churches, etc. This will save you time because you won't have to go back and check to see how something was spelled.

- Create a style guide for your business for editorial decisions about spelling (American, Canadian, British, etc.), treatment of numbers (i.e., spelled out or as numerals), typographical treatments (e.g., are book titles in italics or quotations?), formatting (e.g., are paragraphs flush

TRANSCRIPT TO MANUSCRIPT: COMPARING VERBATIM TRANSCRIPTS AND AN EDITED MANUSCRIPT

Unedited Transcripts:

Sometimes a story is told little by little, at various times over the course of several interviews.

Interview #1:

Q. Did you meet Elizabeth before you joined the army?

A. No, not before. We fell in love before we saw each other.

Q. Really?

A. That sounds odd, doesn't it? But the thing is, my brother Charles … my brother was very sick and he tried to get into the army, navy, or air force but he couldn't get in.

Q. What was he sick with?

A. He had scarlet fever very badly, and he never got over it. So they wouldn't let him in the army, navy, or air force. Wasn't fit. So he had an inn … no, no, no, not an inn. His wife ran a tea room in the village — Agnes. She did the baking. Well I mean they both ran the place. My brother did odd jobs like you know fixing things like taps and he liked talking to the people who'd come for tea and sandwiches. So he — they took in service people. He wanted to contribute something to the war. They'd come to the rooms morning, noon, or night and have a cup of tea, and people in the village saw this and understood this and they'd bring rations …

Q. What kind of rations?

A. Like jam and margarine so they could give them to the troops. They … the service people, they came for fellowship as much as refreshments. One of the people who contributed was my Lizzie. She worked in the kitchen with Agnes, too.

Q. Tell me how you came to fall in love with Elizabeth before meeting her.

A. Well Elizabeth came and my brother was very sick and wasn't able to write very much, so Elizabeth said she'd write to me. So she did. So we fell in love before we saw each other. That's how it happened. And I'm more in love with her now than I've ever been.

Interview #4:

A. I was in the Burma campaign. I got this letter and didn't know who it was from but my brother did write later and said Elizabeth had asked to write me, so of course they said sure. I read and re-read Elizabeth's letter. So — I thought, well, look at that. I pondered over it and as time went on I didn't answer it immediately. I, uh … It was several days before I answered. And the more I read it the more I was drawn to her. She gave me no indication. She simply signed it, her letter, "yours sincerely," no "love" or anything like it. She signed it, "Elizabeth, your unknown friend." So I pondered this letter, wondered about its purpose. And neither she nor I have ever regretted the day we got married.

Q. How long have you been married?

A. Fifty-five years. Fifty-five years. So we've got a lot to be thankful for.

Interview #5:

A. There was something more to it than just a letter. It wasn't … I just didn't know what … I pondered over that letter, I wondered about it, and it became mutual and I didn't know it. I loved her through that letter. Not through that particular letter but as the time went on I did. But our friendship up to that point was purely platonic. We didn't tell each other; we never expressed our love for one another; given the distance it wouldn't be fair. I thought, *Well when I get home I've got to have a talk with this girl.* I had a feeling about her unlike anything I'd experienced in my life. Anyway, that's it, and here we are.

Edited Manuscript:

Relevant parts of the story are extracted from each transcript, re-written for narrative flow, put in context, and placed chronologically within the life story. The narrator's voice is retained.

Chapter 9

Elizabeth, the Love of My Life

Lizzie and I fell in love before we saw each other. That sounds odd, but it's true. It happened while I was stationed in India during the Burma campaign in World War II.

Back in England, Elizabeth had become friends with my brother Charles and his wife Agnes, who ran a small tea room in the village. Charles had had a serious case of scarlet fever, which he never recuperated from, and couldn't join the services; they said he was not fit. But he was still handy. He fixed things around the tea room while Agnes did the baking and served customers. He enjoyed talking to the customers, too; he always had the gift of the gab. He and Agnes wanted to do something for the troops, so they had an open-door policy with the soldiers and air force servicemen who were stationed nearby. Morning, noon, and night, they'd drop in and have some tea and maybe some sandwiches. They came for the fellowship as much as the refreshments. Everything was rationed — butter, milk, margarine, jam — so he and Agnes didn't have much to offer, but people around the village would give a little bit here and a little bit there to share with the troops. Among the people who contributed was Elizabeth. She'd even help out in the kitchen. She got to know Charles and Agnes very well.

Because Charles was sick and wasn't able to write to me very much, Elizabeth offered to write to me for him. In her first letter, she signed herself, "Elizabeth, your unknown friend." I pondered over that letter, I wondered about it, and it was several days before I answered it. And the more I read it the more I was drawn to her. There was something more to it than just a letter.

At first, of course, our friendship was purely platonic, but as we wrote more and more, our feelings deepened. I loved her through her letters, and it became mutual and I didn't know it. We didn't tell each other; we never expressed our love for one another; given the distance it wouldn't be fair. I thought, *Well when I get home I've got to have a talk with this girl.* I had a feeling about her unlike anything I'd experienced in my life.

When I got home to England, Elizabeth and I had a talk and it was obvious that we were meant for each other. It was a very happy experience for me. And here we are, after fifty-five years of marriage. We have a lot to be thankful for. I'm more in love with her now than I've ever been.

Verbatim Transcript:

This is an excerpt from a verbatim transcript conducted with Heather Wineburg, who came to Canada in 1947 and began volunteer work at Pier 21's nursery in 1956. Pier 21 follows transcribing guidelines of Baylor University's Institute of Oral History.

Interview Participant: Heather Wineburg (nee Davis)

Interviewer: Steven Schwinghamer

Reference: 05.08.10HW

Interview Date: August 10, 2005

Location: Pier 21

Original Recording Equipment: Minidisc, Digitally remastered to WAV and MP3, breaks between each cassette tape indicated.

Transcribed By: Lianne Poole

1:04 HW: My mother was the daughter of a Canadian captain in the First World War, and an English nurse in London, and she came to Canada at the end of the war. My mother was born here, she went back and forth every year, and met my father, and he happened to be an English

Officer. Because they went back and forth every year on the Furness-Withy Line. And they met, and got married in 1936. I wasn't born 'til 1940, I think my Mother went to England in 1938 two years after she was married to live permanently. And — my father was in the Merchant Marine, he was an officer, a first officer. His family was highly decorated. His father was the commander of the Elder Dempster Line, he was an OVE as well as a DSC, um eh, a DSO. My father became a squadron leader in the fleet air arm in the defense of Malta, and he was killed in the Mediterranean. He went missing and was declared dead in January, 1942. My brother was born in November, 1941. And he — my father never saw him.

SS: I'm sorry, that was January of 1942 he was —

HW: He — my father was declared dead, and my brother was born in November. Uh, November 21st, 1941. We came to Canada in April, 1947. We flew from Heathrow Airport.

[Pause as interviewer writes]

SS: Now that's unusual. It's early days to be flying —

HW: Yes, well —

03:07 SS: Do you know how the arrangements were made?

HW: No, no, my mother simply decided that she was going to fly. That was it. And, in England, it was a very interesting thing for us. In England we were very, very wealthy [clears throat]. There are a number of titles in the family, and we lived in very good circumstances. But at that — in 1947 England was allowing no money out, and my mother was only allowed to bring fifty pounds. Um and, it put us from a sort of — we went from a very comfortable life, to an uncomfortable life.

SS: Um hum.

HW: Um, we managed alright, we survived quite comfortably, but the point is, that it was a different way of life altogether. And so, her flying would be quite normal for her to — because her family, because her father had his own plane. So it wasn't you know, it wasn't a big deal.

(Pause)

4:15 SS: Returning to Canada, uh, did she return to family here, did she —

HW: She came back, her father's family were in Truro, Nova Scotia, they were in Bible Hill. And um, she came to Halifax, we stayed in Halifax for about six weeks, we rented a house in Hubbards, Nova Scotia, called the Bivouac, which had an interesting history. It has since burned down. I went to see the site of the house when I was here. And then we moved permanently to the Annapolis valley and lived in Saint Ali. And we lived there for — well my grandmother continued to live there until she died in 1983, so you know there was long connection with the Annapolis Valley.

My mother married again in 1951 to Thomas Morrow, and [pause] she had — the brother I was with was from the second family, they lived In Halifax because he worked there — here in Halifax, and I came up to stay with them. I um — when I was fifteen I was very ill, I had a ruptured appendix and the pneumonia, in those days it was a disastrous situation, and I was very ill for a couple of years. And it was in that period, in 1956, that [pause], that I heard about the volunteer work at the port nursery, and I volunteered um, for the port nursery.

HW: And I came down, and they gave me a blue uniform with a red cross on it and a white headscarf with a red cross on it and I changed, and that was the beginning of the work. [pause] and —

left or indented?), etc. Refer to the *Chicago Manual of Style*, the authoritative text for document preparation.

- Keep the narrator's voice intact by not changing, unnecessarily, the words, phrases, cadence, tone, speech mannerisms ("Gosh," or "I swear it was as big as an elephant's ear"), syntax, and coined words.

- Use formatting creatively. If the narrator tells a joke, for instance, you might consider putting the punch line on a new line.

- Use a mix of sentence structure and sentence length for variety.

If the muse strikes on this first pass and you think of clever, logical, descriptive chapter headings or paragraph headings, put them in.

Find a method or organizing that works for you. One way would be to color-code content according to broad topics such as Birth and Roots, Childhood, Places Lived, Mother, Father, Siblings, Family Life, Toys and Games, Travels, etc., with a catch-all section to be dealt with later for bits and pieces that don't fit into a category. I sometimes put these at the end of the manuscript in a section called Thoughts on … , or Reflections.

Another method would be to copy and paste sections into folders for your topics. For instance, take a few pages where the narrator talks about his childhood and put it into that folder. Later on, 50 pages later, he talks again about his childhood, so you'd copy and paste that section into the same folder, and so on.

After you have your material organized into sections that belong together, you'll do another edit to make them flow. Then you'll do another edit to put all the sections together. Soon, you'll have something resembling a real live manuscript!

5.4 Polish

Once you have the text organized how you want it, read it over again with a very critical eye. Check and correct spelling and grammar. Look at it with a storyteller's eye. Are there places where it lags? Could you eliminate some words or paragraphs that aren't necessary? Are there awkward phrases you could smooth out? Could you make it more powerful somehow, perhaps substituting some words or giving something its own "space"? Are there places you want to ask your narrator to review and clarify? Eliminate repetitions and cut bland material that doesn't add anything to the story. This draft will go to your client so you want it to be as polished as possible.

5.5 Client review of first draft

Your client will be thrilled to see the manuscript. Even though you'll call it the first draft, it's probably actually your third draft. When you deliver it, give the client clear instructions on how you want him or her to make the changes. Explain how you organized the material and how you edited it and polished it. Tell the client how to find the places where you need input. Ask him or her to verify dates, names, and places. If you have added material, ask if he or she wants to include it. For instance, your narrator talked about going to a favorite park in his hometown. When you were checking the spelling of the park, you discovered the man it was named after lived on the same street as your narrator. Does he want to add a sentence such as, "I later learned that Penham Park was named after Jack Penham, who lived just up the street from us."

Tip: Ask your client not to use Microsoft Word's Track Changes tool; I have found this can create problems when clients aren't experienced computer users. If they are making changes electronically, on the Word document, ask them to go ahead and make the change, then highlight where they have changed it. Better yet, give them a hard copy, double- or triple-spaced, with very wide margins that allow them to write their changes right on the paper. The problem with the hard-copy method is that you often can't make out their handwriting. It's time-consuming to sit with them and go over every change, but sometimes this is the most efficient method in the long run.

At this stage, your narrator should not be adding substantial amounts of text or suddenly remembering he forgot to tell the story of how Uncle Bob landed in the clinking and that it must be included. Even small amounts of extra text result in a good amount of work for you, editing and fitting it into the written manuscript. Heaven forbid they want to record more; this involves you transcribing, too. Your contract should have allowed for a certain number of hours to incorporate your clients' changes after the first draft, and how much you charge for any time over that limit. Remind them gently of your agreed-upon number of hours and then stick to it.

The client review stage can take several months or even a year or longer. This is often the case if more than one family member gets involved in the review, or if the narrator has fallen ill. You'll be wanting to move on with the project, but you just have to be patient.

Many factors influence the client review stage. For instance:

- If the client is elderly, most likely a family member will also be involved, and opinions may differ. Try to have one family member as your contact who will act as the final reviewer. You do not want to be put in the position of mediator.

- Facts may need to be verified. It can take time to contact people or find supporting documents. Offer to help if your client seems unsure how to resolve questions.

- People go on vacation. Use the time to take a break yourself, do some marketing, or work on another project.

- The storyteller has second thoughts about what was said about Uncle Phil. Again, offer your opinion and suggestions, but ultimately it's the client's choice.

- Reading the manuscript has sparked other memories. Ask the client to jot down memories or stories that he or she wants to add. Charge accordingly.

- A client may feel a finality about it and not want to let go. This is a natural reaction. Most times, the client has enjoyed the interviewing process. Assure him or her that an update can be done whenever he or she wants, and that your relationship need not come to a complete halt once the project is finished.

There are a few ways to handle the client review stage:

- Manage expectations right from the start and avoid surprises. Once you start to edit the manuscript, show the client a sample chapter or two along with the relevant transcript. This allows him or her to see your style and the extent to which you'll be editing their words. Clear up any misunderstandings before you invest too much time.

- Think about putting something in your contract along the lines of: "Client will make every effort to return the first draft within a reasonable time, not to exceed three months."

- If the review is just not happening, for whatever reason, offer to sit with the client and go over the manuscript with him or her. The client may be quite happy to do it that way. Charge your normal hourly rate.

This stage is not something you can rush, so don't even try. Remember that this process is likely one of the most important tasks in your client's life, if not the most important, so give him or her breathing space while you move on to another project.

Use this time to take a deep breath and congratulate yourself knowing you've completed 85 percent of the project. Remember to keep your records up-to-date. Record how much time you spent on the project, how much you've been paid and how much is still due, and make yourself a reminder about when to contact the client and ask about progress on the review. Don't forget about the client; call or email within a week or so of delivering it and ask if they have any questions.

You also might consider putting a clause in your contract that states if the client review takes longer than a certain amount of time, you will be paid in full immediately.

When the manuscript comes back, you'll have changes to make. Do not take it personally if the client removed the little gems you inserted, and do not judge the client if they took out what you felt was his or her best story. It's your client's book. You are merely the conduit for the story.

After you make the changes, I strongly recommend you hire a copyeditor to give it a final once-over (or more likely a twice-over) for grammar, style, spelling (please don't even think of relying on your computer's spell check), punctuation, typos, consistency, and so on. A second pair of eyes is essential and worth every penny.

Once you've delivered a final copy to your client, pat yourself on the back, again. Another life has gone into the world's storybook, thanks to you. Cash your check and treat yourself.

5.6 Editing a manuscript that's already written

If editing and writing is your strength, you can market yourself as a specialist in memoirs. Imagine the hundreds of partially-written memoirs begging to be finished and properly preserved! You'll probably charge by the hour for this. One method of estimating the cost is to see how long it takes you to edit five to ten pages, then simply multiply that time by the number of pages in the manuscript. Be sure to add some time for a review.

When you give the client the estimate, make it clear that it is an estimate. Sometimes it's not until you start editing that you realize the project's going to take longer than you originally thought. In that case, alert the client that the final cost may be higher than what you quoted.

Be extremely liberal in your cost and time estimates. Communicate clearly and often, so there are no surprises.

6. Book Production

Though some clients are content to just have a manuscript written, and perhaps coil-bound by the local print shop, most people want the manuscript published along with family photos. If, once the client has approved the final manuscript, he or she wants to proceed with a book, you have a fun and challenging time ahead of you. At this point you know your narrator's life story inside and out. Shepherding his or her (and your) words through the design, layout, printing, and binding of a book is a wonderfully satisfying experience.

I do encourage clients to go the whole nine yards and publish the manuscript. Sometimes it's just not in their budget — it is not an inexpensive undertaking — and while there's always talk of "sometime in the future" I always wonder if it will really happen or the manuscript is doomed to languish in a dusty corner cupboard.

6.1 First step: The vision

Talk to the client about his or her likes and dislikes. Again, sometimes this is determined by budget, but in initial talks, try to "blue sky" it and establish the vision. It really helps to have some sample books, if not your own, then books in several sizes, covers, layouts, and so on. Even if you have your own sample, show the client a few other books so he or she can see what's possible.

6.2 Custom design

Book design is an art. By the time a personal history project reaches the book production stage, a lot of heart and soul has gone into it, so it deserves to be showcased in an attractive, elegant design that will stand the test of time. Book designers use their skills and experience to determine and implement the best choices for size, format, paper, fonts, the look and feel, cover treatment, colors, photo treatments, and page layouts. They also handle special features such as sidebars, quotes, or maps. They can do the photo and document scans and touch-ups, find complementary photos on the Internet, and usually know some reliable printers and binders. A good design can enhance the reader's appreciation of the story; a bad design can detract from it.

A designer's fee is one of the biggest variables in the cost of book production, so if you do decide to hire one, shop around. Ask to see portfolios, and get quotes from at least three companies. Provide each designer with a few pages of text and a couple of photographs, and ask them to show you a suggested layout. Depending on the client's wishes, you may want to show your client the three styles and let him or her choose the one he or she likes best.

6.3 Do it yourself

6.3a Layout programs

If the cost of a professional book designer is too high, you could do it yourself if you have some design experience and skills (or are willing to invest a lot of time acquiring them). No one is more intimately familiar with the storyteller and the story than you, so you can use your creative juices to bring your client's personality into the pages of the book. The "gold standard" of layout software is Adobe's InDesign, but it's expensive and has a pretty steep learning curve. There are other programs, including Apple's Pages. It doesn't have the breadth of features of InDesign, but the learning curve is shorter; it's easier to use and may be adequate for your client's book. Doing layout with Microsoft Word is possible, but not recommended. Before you start, talk to a printer to make sure you're setting up your layout properly. Most printers and binders will be happy to give advice and suggestions. Some will give you samples of paper and covers.

At this point, you can have it printed and bound by local companies or send it to one of the online print-on-demand digital publishing services as described in the next section.

6.3b Print-on-demand (POD) digital publishing

An affordable option is to use a print-on-demand (POD) publisher such as Blurb, Lulu, CreateSpace, or another. They are called POD because they use digital printing to produce books only as they are ordered, unlike traditional offset or letterpress printing that made small runs prohibitively expensive. With POD you can order any number of books — even one, if that's all you require. The quality is good and is more than adequate for the average customer. Its technology and choices are becoming more sophisticated. For many projects, this is an excellent option that will satisfy a good percentage of clients.

With these POD services, you can either upload your own already-laid-out pages that you created with InDesign or another layout program, or use a template provided by the POD publisher. A template is a page that's set up to a certain size, with space for text and photographs. You insert your text (you can copy and paste from Word) and photographs, move things around, play with fonts and styles, design a cover with image wrap (an image wrapping around the front and back cover) or dust jacket (the glossy paper that covers the cover), and even replace their logo with your own business logo. Once you're happy with everything, you upload your book file. The book is printed, bound, and delivered to your door in a matter of weeks. You don't pay for the software, only for the books themselves. The price per book is quite reasonable, and you can choose from several sizes, softcover or hardcover options, black and white or color, and a wide variety of page layout templates.

A bonus is that once the book is printed, some companies let you set up a "store" on their websites. This means that family or friends can order the book themselves and don't need you or your client as the go-between.

6.4 Book decisions

Whether you hire a designer or do it yourself, some of the decisions to be made by you (and your client) about the book are:

- Size and orientation (portrait or landscape)

- Number of photographs and if they'll be in color or black and white

- Photo placement: will photos be interspersed throughout the book, or bundled together in a special section, perhaps printed on a glossy stock photos, in the middle of the book? This makes the book layout simpler and therefore saves money.

- Number of copies

- Hardcover or softcover?

- Dust jacket/cover photo and other cover treatments?

- What kind of binding?

- What kind of cover? Cloth (linen), leather, an image printed right on the cover?

Whichever way you choose — designing it yourself, hiring someone, using POD or even just your local print shop — get a couple of sample pages to show your client and get his or her approval in writing. Once the book is laid out, proofread it again carefully. Better yet, hire a proofreader for a fresh pair of eyes. If you're ordering several copies of the book, print one copy first for your proof copy and examine it carefully before giving the go-ahead to print several copies and deliver them to your client.

Tip: For the beginner and intermediate non-designer, Robin Williams' *The Non-Designer's Design Book* (Berkeley: Peachpit Press, 1994) is an excellent guide to good design.

6.5 Photos

6.5a Photo selection

Sitting down with your client to choose photos to go in the book is fun! The right photos can enhance the stories immeasurably and make a book visually exciting. They are always a great memory-prompter when conducting interviews, too.

- A photo of a person can show a great deal about his or her temperament and personality.

- It can surprise a grandson when he sees himself in his grandfather's face (so that's where the red hair came from!).

- A visual experience can elicit emotions in a different way than words can. You can look deeply into a photo and use your own imagination to create a story around it.

- A photograph of a neighborhood store can bring back a flood of memories about penny candy, spending allowances, a first job, and so on.

- A photo of a Christmas dinner brings smiles and memories and prompts discussion of where it was taken and who was there. Was that the year the tree fell over?

- Photos tell about fashions, trends, and social behavior.

- I'm not sure whether a photo is worth 1,000 words, but a lot of a story can be told in a photo and its caption, which can be written in third person so it allows for a more factual and all-encompassing perspective. You can add bits of historical interest. For instance, if there's a picture of the narrator's father in his military uniform, along with identifying the father you could add something about obligatory military training in Switzerland.

Sometimes you can find an image online that would be great to include, for instance, a photo of the hometown of the narrator's grandmother. In all instances when using photographs found on the Internet or from another source, you must secure written permission if the source does not explicitly state that the image is copyright-free. Copyright-free means it is in the public domain and that anyone can use it. Royalty-free is not the same thing. That just means you don't have to pay a royalty fee to use it.

6.5b Handling old photos

Proper handling of old, fragile photographs and documents is vitally important. The last thing you want to do is damage your client's precious and irreplaceable items! Before you face this situation, do some research — a lot of research — on best practices. If you can give your client some practical advice for ongoing storage and restoration, all the better. I am not an expert in this field, but this overview is meant to alert you to areas for further research:

- Hold photos and documents at the edges, supporting them with two hands.

- Wear white cotton gloves to keep your skin's oils from touching the surface.

- Keep photographs covered when they are not being viewed. Sunlight is very damaging.

- Do not use pen to write on the back of the photograph. Use a soft lead pencil.

- If documents and photos are too fragile to even lay on a scanner bed, take a photograph instead.

6.5c Scanning photos and documents

If you're hiring a designer, he or she could scan the photos, but if he or she lives far away, or to save money, you may want to scan the photos yourself and send them electronically to your designer. I would never trust the mail service with priceless family photos, especially if they're not mine!

Scanning photos and documents takes skill and knowledge, more than most people realize. It's one thing to scan the family reunion photo for the purpose of emailing it to your relatives, whereas scanning for inclusion in an heirloom book is a whole new ballgame. Invest in some training, and with practice, you can do a good job yourself. (For an excellent source of information see www.scantips.com.)

Resolution: For print purposes, you need to scan at at least 300 dpi (dots per inch), and even higher for tiny old photos that you want to make larger. For instance, if you scan a 2 inch x 2 inch photo at 300 dpi, you can't print that as a 5 inch x 7 inch and keep the same resolution as the quality of the photo will be greatly diminished in the printed book. Scan small photos at least at 600 dpi.

Format: It's best to save your photos in TIFF, which stands for Tag Image File Format. This format does not compress your files into a smaller size, which compromises quality by reducing the amount of detail in the image. The popular JPG format uses lossy compression, which makes it a smaller format, but it also loses quality. JPG is fine for websites and emails, and takes up less space on your computer, but the quality is not usually good enough for a printed book. If space on your hard drive is an issue, you might want to invest in an external hard drive for photo storage, as TIFF files are very large.

Stay organized: Set up a good filing system right from the start. Decide on a naming convention that makes sense to you, such as labeling by family name, date of photograph, theme, chapter the image will go in, etc. For example, for the first photo in Chapter 4 of the McAllister family history, you might name the image: McA07XmasChap4.01. Be consistent for all the photos and illustrations for the whole project.

How to charge: When you're quoting a price to scan a client's photos, keep in mind that the job entails a lot more time than merely placing the photo on the scanning bed and pressing a couple of buttons. Take all the following into account when calculating the amount of time you'll need:

- Will the client give you the photos, or are you expected to help with the selection?

- Do you need to extract the photos from an album?

- Volume: how complex will your filing system need to be?

- Will you need to do additional research to identify the people or places in the photos?

- Captions might seem like little things, but you'll be surprised at how much time they can eat up when writing, checking names and dates and relevant information, and editing for space.

What if a client tells you he knows about a place that will scan photos for 50 cents each? Do enough research so you can explain to him or her the difference between what those bulk places do and what you can do for him. And, does he really want to trust his precious photos to a large company handling thousands of photos, or worse yet, does he want to send them off in the mail?

Tip: Gently wipe your scan bed every few scans. It's amazing how much dust it gathers and how those minute little specs of dust show up on an image.

6.5d Photo enhancement and editing

Editing, manipulating, cropping, and especially restoring photos are parts of an area that, if you have the budget, is great to hand over to an expert. However, with some practice, you can probably do much of this yourself with a photo-editing program such as Photoshop or its "lite" version, Photoshop Elements. It's easy to get carried away once you learn all the nifty tricks and special effects, but restrain yourself or you'll be fiddling with the photos into next year. Probably the most useful tools of photo-editing software are for cropping, balancing the tone with the Levels adjustment, balancing color with the Color Balance adjustment, cleaning up stains or discolorations, and maybe removing the telephone pole sticking out of Granddad's head.

One school of thought says not to retouch old photos at all; that by doing so you lose the authenticity and charm of days gone by. My advice is to do some gentle touch-up if the photo is so far gone that it's hard to recognize a face or important element. Usually, I lean toward a minimal amount of fuss.

Tip: One bad (fuzzy, too dark, or too light), unfixable photo can affect the aesthetics of the whole page, so avoid it if you can. If a photo has great sentimental value and the client really wants to include it, try to minimize its impact, perhaps by the cropping or placement.

6.6 Printing and binding options

Familiarize yourself with the best printing and binding methods so that you can explain them to your client. There are a wide range of options, depending on budget and the desired format. For instance, for a family cookbook you might want to choose coil binding so the book can lay flat as the chef prepares a recipe.

Just about anything is possible, from very inexpensive options, to custom printed endpapers, to a medallion or other memento embedded in a leather cover. Get some samples, even if you didn't produce them yourself, to show your client.

There are many publishers that produce limited edition books, which are surprisingly affordable, too. They can assist with all aspects of manuscript preparation if you want to hand everything over to them.

6.6a Working with printers

Once you've determined the specifications of your book — the size, format, type of cover, paper stock, number of photos, number of pages, etc. — get at least three quotes based on those specifications. Be willing to consider suggestions from the printers, too. Ask to see a sample of the printer's work, and ask questions. If they're using a lot of technical terms or lingo you don't understand, stop them and ask for explanations in layperson's language. You not only want to assess whether they know what they're talking about; you're looking for someone you want to do business with. There may be (in fact, probably will be) some snags: last minute changes, unavailability of a particular type of endpaper, or postal or courier delays. A good relationship will help you weather such complications and maintain a friendly business arrangement, and it will get easier and smoother the longer you work together.

6.6b Making it special

Suggest to your client that he or she orders at least one hardcover copy in an elegant presentation box — a custom-made clamshell box or slipcase that not only looks great, but helps protect the book (and/or CDs or DVDs) during handling, transportation, and storage.

6.6c Hand-binding

Bookbinding is a time-honored craft. Consider visiting a hand-binder to see how he or she works. If you get excited at the thought of creating gorgeous hand-bound books yourself, take a bookbinding course and add unique, one-of-a-kind books to your product line. Do an Internet search for schools and institutions that offer classes. Try searching "book arts" as well as "bookbinding."

Tip: With the right training and experience in book arts, you could specialize and offer services in restoration and repair of old diaries, cookbooks, photo albums, atlases, antique books, local histories, business archives, rare books, military histories, and Bibles.

7. Producing a CD

As a personal historian, you're in a position to capture one of the most meaningful sounds in the world: the voice of a loved one as he or she shares the stories of his or her life. Hearing a voice can transport us in time and place, and it becomes even more precious if the storyteller is no longer with us, so understandably, a CD recording of the storyteller is a vital component of the personal history.

7.1 The audio recording as the end product

Some personal historians work only in audio — interviewing the narrator and burning the recordings onto CDs. Some editing may be done to eliminate long silences, and tracks can be made and labelled, like on a DVD movie, so the listener can easily find a certain segment. Audacity is a free audio-editing software program, and there are many more reasonably priced ones.

You can package your CDs in an attractive case with a custom-designed label.

The advantages of working in audio are:

- It's much more affordable than transcribing, editing, and publishing a book.

- It captures the voice of the narrator complete with laughter, emotion, accents, song, and speech mannerisms that are difficult if not impossible to convey in print.

- With the proper training, it's relatively fast and easy to do a personal history.

The disadvantages are:

- A CD or DVD may not be usable in the future and it will be up to someone in the family to transfer the sound file to a new format and keep up with changing technology.

- A book or even a manuscript is a tried and tested format. Plus, photographs can be added to enhance the story. Story and photos are kept together in one place.

- Most (some?) people find it easier to open a book than insert a CD into a playing device.

- Reading a book — especially one about a relative — is an intimate experience. Without the use of headphones, listening to a CD is a more public experience than reading a book.

Whether or not you work only in audio or, as I do, work with the printed word and the audio recordings, you will have to upload your recordings onto your computer.

Thanks to technology, here's what I do after an interview:

1. Use a USB cord to plug my digital recorder into my computer.

2. An icon appears on my desktop. I open it by clicking on it, and there, bless the techies of the world, are my audio files.

3. I make a new folder on my desktop and copy the files into that folder, which I aptly name using the client's last name and the date of the interview.

4. After following my recorder's instructions for safe unplugging, I can unplug it and turn it off.

5. I now have the files on my computer.

I record in .wav files, which are large but better quality than some other formats, so I use iTunes to make a smaller .mp3 version, which is the one I send to my transcriber either as an email attachment or through a service like YouSendIt or DropBox which, for a reasonable fee or sometimes even free of charge, allows you to send media files that are too big for normal email. Magic!

8

THE INTERVIEW — THE HEART OF PERSONAL HISTORY

Interviewing is both an art and a science. The *science* of good interviewing is that it requires a strong skill set honed by trial and error, and uses definite techniques to elicit the best responses from a subject (to the degree that one can prove what is the "best" response). The *art* of interviewing is in developing your own style that will work. It's about using intuition and creatively conducting and shaping the interview session so that it almost takes on a life of its own.

One of the most important questions you should ask yourself as you interview your narrator is: What do I want to discover about this person?

It is possible for anyone to press an "on" button and ask some questions. It's how you ask them and what you ask, and the rapport you build with your narrator that will determine the difference between a mediocre story and a special story.

1. What Makes a Good Interview?

1.1 You can lead a horse to water ...

It's vital that you capture as much information as possible, and the right information — the stuff that your narrators want to tell, the stories the families treasure, stories of historical importance — whatever the focus is. Having said that, you can only elicit whatever your narrator is willing to share. Pushing or prodding will get you nowhere and may in fact alienate your storyteller and cause him or her to clam up.

This is why it's important that the narrator is "on board" with the interviews from the start. The rest of the family may want the narrator to tell certain aspects of his or her life story but he or she might not want to.

A story to illustrate this: A daughter hired me to get her father's story, and he reluctantly agreed. As we began, he told me most definitely that he would not talk about his feelings about anything. He'd describe events and places and other stories, but he was just not into that "touchy-feely" stuff. Knowing that, I steered clear of those types of questions and the interview went well.

So, respect the wishes of the narrator. If there's a large gap between what the family wants (if they are the ones paying you) and what the narrator wants, it's best to discuss this prior to the start of the project.

1.2 A safe and open environment

Here are a few problem/solution scenarios that might hamper the kind of open, honest environment you want for interviews, and how you might handle them:

- **The narrator is afraid something he or she says will hurt someone:** Talk about parameters before you begin. Assure the subject from the start that he or she will have complete control over the content that goes into the book. Tell him or her you can also edit out sections of the audio. I encourage the storyteller to make this his or her book or CD and to say whatever he or she wants to say, but to also realize that the book may be read by other family members, both now and in the future. I don't believe that a memoir should be a vehicle for vitriol or hateful comments. Saying a brother-in-law "never amounted to much" or

was a "good-for-nothing" is fine; that's the narrator's perspective and it may well be true. Saying the brother-in-law stole from his wife is another matter. That's a harsh accusation and though it might be true, if it's not true the narrator could be sued for libel. Also, remind your narrator that such statements may be directed at the brother-in-law, but his memoir may be read by that man's children. Does he really want to take the chance that people could be hurt? Derogatory stories about other people say more about the narrator than the people he or she is talking about. It can come across as mean-spirited and petty, and may well be regretted one day. I think it's your responsibility to at least offer advice to your client. But in the end, it is the client's book. As long as you protect yourself from a lawsuit in your contract, it's largely beyond your control.

- **The narrator may be afraid of dredging up painful episodes:** Assure the narrator that he or she needs only to talk about what he or she wants to. Tell the narrator if he or she doesn't want to answer your question, to just say so. Be attuned to signals, though, and be ready to follow up on small openings into areas that the narrator is slowly venturing into. The memory may be too raw one day, but another day he or she might be willing to try to process it.

- **You remind the narrator of a nasty teacher from the past:** It's true that sometimes there's simply a clash of personalities or an irrational (or subconsciously rational, if that's possible) reason that you don't get along. There's not much you can do if the narrator just doesn't like your red hair and green eyes or whatever physical thing it is that triggers a reaction. If it truly becomes a problem, you can either grin and bear the frosty atmosphere and finish the interviews, or bow out of the project. (See more about difficult clients in Chapter 14, section **2.6**.)

- **He or she is afraid of offending you:** As much as possible, keep your own personality out of the process. You're not there to make a friend. Your job is to guide the narrator through the telling of his or her own truth. Keep your experiences to yourself, as much as you might be tempted to share a similar story to the one just told to you. Park your own values at the door. But again, you have to make the call if you find the narrator simply too hateful to work with. It can happen. It would have to be an extreme circumstance, but if you find yourself with a client who's revealing things that are so at odds with your own code of ethics (I'm thinking of revelations of murder, rape, incest, torture, or bullying), it might be best to bow out.

- **The narrator is afraid of shocking you and you know he or she is holding back:** While you're only human, try your best to remain neutral. Your narrator may want to "protect" you from the nastiness of the world, as you may remind him or her of a son or daughter. Sometimes you'll hear stories he or she has never told anyone else — maybe for good reason. The fact that he or she is telling these to you is a testament to your rapport — you are trusted; he or she feels it is safe to say anything in front of you. For this reason, it's important not to show your feelings on your face or through body language, like immediately crossing your arms and legs and getting yourself in a closed-up knot! If your narrator genuinely likes you, he or she may subconsciously not want to hurt you or expose you to shockingly brutal stories, such as those carried inside Holocaust survivors. Assure him or her at the beginning of the interviews, perhaps not in so many words, that you are used to hearing all kinds of stories, that your clients often cry, and that sometimes you'll cry with them. It's as simple as that. Once it's out in the open that there are going to be emotional moments, it might clear the air. During the interview, if your narrator is too upset to continue, ask if he or she wants to take a break.

- **The narrator may simply be worried that he or she is boring you and has nothing worthwhile to talk about:** Be interested and act interested.

- **He or she is worried about his or her storytelling ability:** Assure the narrator that you will pull the bits and pieces together, and "story" doesn't have to mean a full narrative with a beginning, middle, and end. You want to hear even brief vignettes and anecdotes, or even a memory "out of the blue," such as about a Halloween costume.

Tip: Know your limits. If you feel that your interview sessions are turning into therapy sessions and your narrator is getting dangerously upset or delving into waters best dealt with by a trained therapist, discuss it with the family or the narrator.

2. Pre-Interview Preparation

Good planning before you begin the interviews will save you time, make the process more efficient, and involve your client and narrator right from the start.

2.1 How many, how long, how often

2.1a Eight is great

The number of hours you spend with a client might be determined by his or her budget, but if this is not a big issue, I suggest you try to secure at least eight hours for one narrator's whole life story.

2.1b Try for two

Talk to your narrator about how long he or she wants each session to be. I recommend you keep interviews to two hours or less, though allow for longer if it's going well and the narrator wants to continue. Sometimes it's best to limit interviews to an hour or 90 minutes. In the "old days" when cassette recorders were used, 90 minutes was the length of both sides of a cassette, so it was a natural place to stop for the day. With a digital recorder, you can carry on for hours — but you wouldn't want to under normal circumstances.

2.1c Give me a break

Talk about how often you'll meet. Everyone's different, and there might be circumstances such as limited time due to terminal illness, but in general I think it's good to have a meeting once every seven to ten days or so. This gives you and your client time to step back and think about what you talked about, for you to get the transcribing done, and for the narrator to perhaps delve into the family albums now that he or she is reviewing the past, which could lead to more memories and stories. Also, you may be balancing several clients' needs, interviewing two days per week, and editing or project managing the rest of the time. You want to give yourself time to attend to other work areas.

2.2 Time and place

Before your first interview session, by email, telephone, or in person, set up a time and place that's mutually convenient. Ask your client if there's a certain day of the week that is not good for him or her; perhaps it's the day the cleaning lady comes (you don't want a vacuum cleaner roaring in the background). Make a note of this in your business diary. As well, determine the best time of day. Some elderly or ill people get very tired after lunch, so mornings may be preferable. Other people will be at their best in the afternoons.

2.3 Information gathering

Ask your client to provide some factual information by filling out a biographical information form. It should include:

- full name and address,

- contact information of other family members if they are involved in the project,

- parents' and grandparents' names and the dates of their births and deaths, if known,

- names of their children and when and where they were born,

- major places lived,

- education,

- career, and

- hobbies, travels, and other highlights he or she wants to cover in the interviews.

Having this documented not only ensures that you have the correct spelling and facts; it gives you an idea of what's important to the client. It also gives you some background information that will be a jumping-off point for your research into where he or she lived, what was going on in the world at certain times in his or her life, and anything else that will help you develop intelligent questions for the interviews. For an example biographical information form, see Sample 13.

Also, ask the family members, if they're involved, to provide you with a list of topics or stories about which you should ask the narrator, like a marriage proposal or an award-winning speech. The narrator might not even think to bring that up, and if you don't know about it, neither will you.

3. Structuring the Interviews

As you structure the interviews, you'll want to bear in mind what the final product will be. Although there's a lot of crossover, there are definite differences between interviews conducted for audio-only (the interviews on a CD), a lightly-edited transcript, and a fully edited narrative.

3.1 Audio-only (interviews on CD)

If you are specializing in audio, with the client buying the CDs of the interviews, you'll want the best recording equipment you can afford and the optimal setting for recording. It's vital that you have a quiet environment. You will want to keep your own voice to a minimum, but your questions must be loud and clear enough to understand, otherwise the answers will not make sense. For this product, I do recommend that you provide your clients with a list of general topics for the interviews, so they can start to think about answers. This will, hopefully, give you a smoother narration. You'll also want to ask questions in a logical order (chronologically would be the most popular choice) and keep the client on track to answer those specific questions.

Tip: If a client is very elderly or infirm, CDs alone may not be the ideal product. He or she may ramble, speak nonsensically, go off on tangents, and otherwise be hard to listen to, and even major audio editing will not give a pleasing life story. Although the recordings will still be precious to the family, your client may also wish to engage you to transcribe the recordings and make sense of the stories.

3.2 Transcript or lightly-edited transcript

Some clients will just want a lightly-edited transcript. This is still in a question-and-answer format, but has been edited to eliminate the "ums" and "ers," broken sentences, false starts, etc. When planning the interviews for this product, you will save yourself a lot of time and effort by asking questions in order and keeping the narrator on track.

Because your questions will be included in the transcript, you'll want to make them as complete as possible, worded in a way that will make sense on a transcript. For instance, if you know some of the personal background, you could ask a question like, "You grew up in a very large family. What was it like being the youngest?"

3.3 Fully edited manuscript or book

A fully edited manuscript or book gives you the most freedom during interviews, because the narrator can go off on as many tangents as he or she wants. (Often, this leads in a roundabout way to more memories or details.) You'll be extracting whatever you need to make complete sentences, paragraphs, chapters, etc. For instance, if the narrator jumps from his golf game to when he learned to drive to his wedding and back to his golf game, you can let him, knowing that you will eventually be putting

BIOGRAPHICAL INFORMATION FORM

Name _____
   (First)   (Middle)   (Last)

Address _____
   (Street)   (City)

   _____
   (Province or State)   (Postal Code or Zip Code)

Alternate
Residence _____
   (Street)   (City)

   _____
   (Province or State)   (Postal Code or Zip Code)

Date of Birth _____

Place of Birth _____

Paternal Grandparents

Name	Date/Place of Birth	Date/Place of Death	Occupation

Maternal Grandparents

Name	Date/Place of Birth	Date/Place of Death	Occupation

Parents

Name	Date/Place of Birth	Date/Place of Death	Occupation

Step-Parents (if applicable)

Name	Date/Place of Birth	Date/Place of Death	Occupation

Siblings

Name	Date/Place of Birth	Date/Place of Death	Occupation

Spouse(s)

Name	Date/Place of Birth	Date/Place of Marriage	Occupation

Children (including step-children)

Name	Date/Place of Birth	Current Residence

Grandchildren

Name	Date/Place of Birth	Current Residence

Education

School	Location	Dates

_____

_____

_____

_____

_____

Employment/Business

Employer/Company Name	Dates	Job Title	Location

_____

_____

_____

_____

_____

Dwelling Locations

List major places you have lived, starting with childhood.

Location	Dates

_____

_____

_____

_____

_____

Special Memories

Your interviewer will be asking about the unique experiences in your life. To be sure that the most important aspects are covered, please note here any special events, persons, or other items you definitely want included in your memoir. These might include family traditions, favorite family stories, special pets, holidays, relationships, etc.

_____

_____

_____

_____

_____

Significant Events

What relationships and/or events shaped your life (e.g. if X hadn't happened, my life would have taken a different turn): illness, death, birth, trauma, special people, marriage, career choice, religious/spiritual experience, etc.?

_____

_____

_____

_____

_____

_____

Clubs and Civic Organizations

Name	Dates	Location	Your Activities

_____

_____

_____

_____

Military Service

Branch of Service   Dates Served

_____

_____

_____

_____

Hobbies/Recreation

How do you like to relax or spend your time?

_____

_____

_____

_____

_____

Travel

Please list major travels, including dates.

_____

_____

_____

_____

_____

_____

_____

Interests

Do you have any special interests? Politics, science, art, history, technology, etc.?

_____

_____

_____

_____

_____

_____

_____

all those stories in logical order in the finished manuscript.

You can make these interviews more relaxed and free-form. Even though you'll probably give your clients a CD of the recorded interviews, this is secondary to getting the raw material needed to write the manuscript.

Knowing the family wants a book, you might want to incorporate in your interviews an opportunity for the narrator to show you some photographs and talk about them. Not only might this spark more memories and stories, but you'll have a great head start on writing captions for the photos that will go in the book.

4. Your First Interview with a New Client

So, you have a completed biographical information form and have done some research into the narrator's life and times, such as where he or she grew up, what was happening in the world at that time, etc. You've talked to the family about what stories they want. You know what the family wants for a final product: the interviews on CD, a CD plus transcript, CD plus manuscript, or a published book. You've set up a meeting that's a good time for you and the client. You've determined how many interview hours you'll spend together, or agreed to make your arrangement open-ended. You have a contract and a deposit and everyone understands the process. Finally, you've confirmed the appointment with your narrator.

Time to get talkin'!

4.1 Preparing your client

Here are a few key points to help you prep your narrator:

- Your narrator is probably just as nervous as you are so you need to put him or her at ease. Spend a bit of time just chatting about the house, his or her children, or the weather. Agree on how long you'll stay today. Ask if the narrator has any questions.

- Explain how the recorder works and that he or she needs to speak as clearly and loudly as possible. Remind the speaker that he or she should speak naturally and freely, but to tell the stories as if someone is hearing them for the first time — which you are, of course. The narrator should provide as much backstory and detail as possible — give the story context. For example: "My Uncle Fred — that's my dad's brother — he'd come to live with us when Aunt Ethel died … "

- Tell the narrator to take as much time as needed to answer a question and that you will not rush to fill silences. After a few hours together you might come to know when the narrator is ready to move on or is still thinking about an answer.

- Tell him or her that just because you're not always saying something like "How interesting!" it doesn't mean you're not listening intently. You're just trying to keep your voice to a minimum. In our conversations with people in everyday life, we feel the need to validate what they're saying with some expression like "Yeah?," "Really?," "Oh my gosh," or "You're kidding." You might find it takes practice to keep yourself from interjecting these extraneous phrases.

- Assure the narrator that if he or she can't recall a name, date or place, it can always be added later.

- Ask the speaker to tell you if he or she needs a break or wants to stop for the day, no matter what time it is. And, because he or she will probably feel like your host, assure the narrator that if you need a break, you'll say so.

- Ask if there's any particular place he or she wants to start, and suggest a general format for the interview such as what topics or era you could cover today.

- Make sure he or she is comfortable, physically.

- At the end of the interview, ask the narrator how he or she feels about the session and what might be good to talk about in the next interview.

4.2 Preparing yourself

A successful personal history project depends on a successful interview. And the interview, to a large degree, depends on you. There are certain things you can do to get ready to interview a client.

Don't leave these until the morning of your interview!

- Make sure your equipment is working. Test it. I never rely on batteries. I always plug the recorder into an outlet. For this reason I always have an extension cord in the car. Know the recorder inside and out. Make sure you have enough memory to record without worry. Before you wipe your memory card clean, don't forget to upload any existing recordings to your computer!

- Do your research and familiarize yourself with where the client grew up or any major events the client lived through. For instance, if he or she came down with polio at 35, find out about the disease. Determine what you don't know but should know. A good interviewer is curious and wants to learn about things he or she doesn't know. Not knowing is sometimes the best approach to getting a whole story.

- Dress appropriately. When I first meet a client I dress formal and businesslike. I always take indoor shoes and change into them when I arrive. One school of thought says that an interviewer should not wear "loud" clothes or even flashy jewellery; anything that distracts the storyteller is a no-no. After a number of sessions, I dress according to what my client usually wears. If the client's in heels and pearls, I continue to dress up, but if he or she is in jeans and a sweatshirt, I go a lot more casual.

- Be impeccably groomed.

- Know the route to your client's house and how long it will take you to get there — then allow another half hour.

- Before you head out, make sure you have enough gas in the car.

- Take with you:
  - your recorder and microphone if you're using one (or two)
  - a notebook and at least two pens
  - an extension cord

- the file you've started for your client with the biographical information form, the phone number, and notes/emails up to this point.

- Your business diary for scheduling the next meeting.

- Before the interview, eat enough so that your stomach won't be growling.

- Allow yourself a lot more time than you think you need to get ready.

5. The Interview Environment

The ideal environment is a quiet space with no background noise, comfortable chairs, the right amount of light, and no fear of distractions like a cell phone ringing. (Be sure to turn your own off.) But real life always has some surprises. A grandchild might come to the door expecting to visit with Grandma. A dog can have an accident right beside your foot. A son-in-law can wake up and start rattling pots and pans in the kitchen. Control what you can and be good-natured about the rest.

Whenever possible, do not allow someone else in the room when you're conducting the interview. Others will inevitably interject with their own version of the story or correct the narrator or ask their own questions. They may very well intimidate the narrator, or at the very least inhibit and make the narrator cautious about what he or she is saying.

6. Establishing Rapport

"The greatest compliment that was ever paid me was when one asked me what I thought, and attended to my answer."

— Henry David Thoreau

Establishing a good relationship with your interviewee is crucial. Smile. Use his or her name frequently. Try the simple but powerful "mirroring" technique of copying a person's body language: posture, gestures, and even tone of voice. Studies show that mirroring subconsciously establishes a connection between people. But be subtle about it, otherwise the pair of you will look like a scene from a Marx Brothers movie! Listen carefully, and be sincere in your praise and compliments; people (especially older people) can spot a phony a mile away.

Tip: Be self-assured. If need be, fake it until you feel it. Even if this is your first interview, act as if you've done it a hundred times. Your interviewee needs to feel in good hands and that you're a professional. If you're bumbling around with your equipment, searching for the "on" button, he or she is going to get even more nervous.

7. Listening

If you learn nothing else from this book, I hope you remember the most important aspect of personal history work is listening. It may sound easy, but listening intently is a learned skill and doesn't come naturally. You'll have a lot of things vying for your attention. You'll be thinking of your next questions, wondering if your recorder is really working, thinking about the time, wishing the washing machine wasn't so loud — and in the middle of all this, you have to be giving your interviewee your absolute undivided attention. With the three quarters of your brain that isn't thinking about the time, the washing machine, etc., you'll be listening for the following:

- In case your narrator gets lost and forgets what he or she was talking about, and says, "Sorry, I got distracted. What was your question?" you'd better know.

- Areas that bear further investigation: If a subject is mentioned tantalizingly briefly, make a note to follow up.

Listening helps you create the flow of the interview. The best interview questions are natural segues from the narrator's last thought or point. If you're not listening intently, you'll miss these opportunities.

8. Interviewing techniques

Entire books have been written on best practices for interviewing, and I suggest you read and study some of these and if possible, get some formal training. What follows is a primer that will help ensure your interviews run smoothly and yield good results.

8.1 He said, she said: Achieving balance

Personal historians share a lot with journalists in that we all want to elicit the best quotes from our subjects. We want to go beyond the surface and reach the emotional side of the subject, and we want our interviewees to speak freely and honestly. Try to establish an atmosphere of mutual respect and sharing. Talk enough that your narrator feels that you are giving something of yourself, too, but know when to be silent and ask direct questions.

8.2 Assess your narrator and tailor your questions

It takes some time to know your narrator — whether he or she would respond to a mere "Go!" and talk nonstop for an hour, or whether he or she needs to be constantly prompted by questions. It also takes time to assess how detailed the narrator's memories are, or how easily he or she gets confused. Someone who is very

SAMPLE 14
INTERVIEW TOPICS

As you prepare your list of questions for your subject, make sure you're asking the why, how, and what questions: Why did your family move? How did you feel about it? What was your new neighborhood like? Use your questions as a jumping off point only; your next question should always try to follow up on the subject's last sentence.

Here are just a few of the topics you should consider in a full life story. Use whatever you know about the subject to ask specific questions that are relevant to his or her life and times.

Ancestors:

Grandparents and Parents:

Family:

Early Childhood:

Youth:

Adulthood:

Parenting years:

School days, elementary and high school:

Military service, if applicable:

Friends:

Relationships with family members, friends, teachers, co-workers, children, grandchildren, spouse:

Historical and world events:

Life experiences:

First job, subsequent jobs, career choices:

Travels:

Self-image, personality, physical characteristics, and character traits:

Retirement activities:

Interests and Hobbies:

Philosophies, values, beliefs (see also Chapter 15, Section **1.1** on ethical wills):

A message to loved ones and future generations:

sharp can handle a two-part question such as, "Why did you choose that college, and do you think you made the right decision?" When you're dealing with a person with some memory loss or who has difficulty staying on track, you will want to ask simple questions, one at a time.

Never think that you'll just "wing it." Always have a list of questions. See Sample 14 for some interview topic ideas.

8.3 Fear not the silence

Do not rush to fill what you think are awkward silences. You'll be amazed at what the narrator will add to what you think was a complete answer. When faced with silence, a rookie interviewer may feel that the subject will think he or she doesn't know what to ask next and jump in with some chatter or another question. Be confident. If, after 30 seconds or so, nothing is forthcoming, simply nod and say, "Okay, let's go on."

After your first few interviews, evaluate yourself. Take a good look at ways you might improve. See Sample 15 for an interview evaluation form; it is also provided on the CD-ROM included with this book so you can print off as many copies as you need.

8.4 Keep it flowing

Don't probe for details when they don't matter to the story. For example, if the narrator starts talking about the time he learned to drive, don't stop his story to ask what kind of car it was or whose car it was. It's distracting and unnecessary. Think of his story as a river that's flowing to the sea; his whole life story being the sea. Some questions that you ask quite innocently might redirect the river or stop the flow and cause a backup. For instance:

Narrator: I remember that first time out in the field, sitting behind the wheel of the car

and feelin' pretty big and important. I was probably about 12 and had to sit way up forward so I could even see past the hood —

You: What kind of car was it? What year?

Narrator: I don't know. Probably a '53.

You: What color was it?

Narrator: I can't remember now. Maybe blue. Yeah, I guess it was blue.

It doesn't matter what year the car was and what color it was. Forget the details and go with the flow.

8.5 Go beyond the surface

8.5a Challenge your narrator

Go beyond the "who, what, when, and where." Some of your best answers will come from the "why" questions.

"You felt you were underpaid. Why didn't you ask for a raise?" "When this person was so rude to you why didn't tell you him off?" "Why didn't you pursue your dream of learning to fly?"

Challenging a narrator about his or her actions can sometimes make you feel cheeky, but your job is to try to get the whole picture, not just the wide brushstrokes. Don't back down from asking those "why" questions just because you keep getting an answer like, "I don't know why I went there. I just did." Eventually something will resonate and you'll get a thoughtful response. At the very least, asking the question will get your client thinking in those terms for the next interview, maybe.

8.5b Open-ended questions

Ask short, open-ended questions like "Tell me more about that." Journalism 101 teaches that the longer the question, the shorter the

SAMPLE 15
INTERVIEW EVALUATION

	YES	NO
Did I record an introduction?		
Did I ask open-ended questions?		
Did I allow silences?		
Did I pick up on unfinished stories and return to them?		
Did I tailor my questions according to the narrator's last points?		
Did I allow my own judgments to color the interview in any way?		
Was the recording clear? Did I set up my equipment properly for the best sound?		
Did I manage the time well? *Did we start and finish on time? Did we cover what I wanted to cover in this session? Did I tell the narrator when we were approaching the end of the interview?*		
Did I thank the narrator for his or her time?		
Did I review the interview when I got home (or heard the recording) and make notes about what to cover in our next session?		

What could I do differently next time to improve my interviewing?

answer. In most cases, don't ask questions that can be answered by just a "yes" or "no."

8.5c Thoughts and feelings

I think the best memoirs are those that balance an account of events, people, places, and things, with a good dose of thoughts, feelings, and reflections. It depends, of course, on what the subject and the family wants, but I've found that for most narrators, it doesn't stop at a factual listing of "and then I did this, and in 1959 we went there." Most people have a lot of wisdom to pass on: life lessons learned, bless-

ings for their families and future generations, etc. (See Chapter 15 for more about how to help clients record these types of messages in ethical wills, or legacy letters.)

8.5d Ups and downs

Try to get the narrator to talk about the down times, too. No life is all roses and chocolate cake. If the narrator keeps talking about how wonderful her childhood was, you might try asking, "Mary, you've shared some great stories about how happy your childhood was. Were there times when you were worried or sad?"

8.6 Assume nothing

Beware of asking loaded questions, such as "I guess with your family being Catholic, that really disappointed your mom?," or making assumptions. If your narrators say something that you don't understand, don't say, "Oh, you mean you wanted to be in the lead role." Instead, ask, "I'm sorry, I don't understand. What do you mean by that?"

Don't anticipate feelings. Take, for instance, a man describing the time his house burned to the ground when he was six years old; his family barely made it out alive. From an adult perspective, it's a horrifying image and our natural reaction is one of sympathy. But as he tells his story, his overwhelming feeling is that it was really exciting. He remembers the fire engines' sirens in the night; being taken into the neighbors' house and given hot chocolate, and new toys to play with. Destruction and panic and loss are not his memory — he remembers the adventure of it all. If he was just starting his story and you jumped in and said, "Oh my God! How horrible," you might inadvertently steer him away from the truth of his memory and he might feel compelled to tell the story from his adult perspective. Stay as neutral as you can and don't insert your own perspective.

8.7 Keeping the focus on your narrator

Most people aren't used to talking about themselves for hours (though they do end up enjoying it). They might deflect attention from themselves by talking about their spouses, neighbors, dog, friends, and most especially, their children, to the point where it feels like it's not about the narrator anymore — it's about how wonderful his or her kids are. As a mom myself, I know that it's hard to break this 20- or 30-year habit, but try to keep the focus on your narrator. Depending on the situation, I might suggest that we devote one entire interview session to the children and grandchildren. The same goes if the narrator is only talking about a wife or husband. This frees him or her up to talk about themselves and not just as a parent, grandparent, spouse, son, daughter, or sibling.

8.8 Keeping on track

It's tough to know when to just let your narrator keep talking. Is it leading to a gem of a memory somewhere out there, or is it just going around in a circle? You don't want to waste time with repetition or tangents that add nothing to the story, such as gossip about an old coworker — wasted time costs your client money. This is when you have to rein in your narrator and get him or her back on track. It's okay to interrupt sometimes. If he or she is telling a story for the third time, unless there's some new information being conveyed, gently interject with, "Yes, I remember you telling me that last week." A more pointed interjection might be, "Sorry to interrupt, John, but I think we've covered your move to New York City. Let's go on to something else. I've been wanting to ask you about ... "

8.9 Interviewing more than one person

For a life history involving a married couple or partnership, a good approach is to dedicate a part of the book to just one person, another part to another person, then a third part about the couple's life together. Conduct separate interviews with each person, then both together. This can work very well — as long as you keep within some guidelines.

On the plus side, partners can help each other remember details, prompt the other to tell a story, and correct each other when they're off track. On the negative side, partners can help each other remember details, prompt the other to tell a story, and correct each other when they're off track.

Yes, that was a deliberate repetition. All the good things about interviewing more than one person can turn into not-so-good things — especially when those people have lived together for many, many years. You've noticed how some couples complete each other's sentences, interrupt, insert their own perspectives, agree for the sake of agreeing, let the other one go first just to be polite … this can be charming and cute, up to a certain point. When it starts interfering with getting a story told completely and honestly, then it's a problem. It's best to have at least some time alone with one spouse, then the other, and then, once the "rules" are established, you can put the microphone between the two of them. Remind them not to talk over each other, and suggest that one person take the lead in answering a certain question, with the other adding his or her perspective.

8.10 Ending an interview

8.10a Wrap it up

Give a 15-minute warning that the interview has to end soon. Try to wrap up any stories that have been started during that interview, while the memories are still fresh.

8.10b End on a positive note

Try not to end a session on an upsetting note or a deeply emotional topic. It's up to you to steer your narrator on to more neutral territory with perhaps some questions like, "Tell me about your all-time favorite meal."

8.11 Special considerations when dealing with the elderly

8.11a Understand limitations

As we age, it's not uncommon to remember our very early years better than later years. Your narrator may have wonderful stories about his childhood but can't remember his second wedding! Try to prompt his memory with photographs, or talk to the family and see if they have some suggestions. If you're being paid by a son or daughter to capture their father's story, keep them informed. Rather than wait until you hand them a manuscript that is much thinner or limited than they anticipated, talk to them about how the interviews are going, how their dad seemed to be feeling, what he talked about, his mood, etc.

8.11b Treat them royally

Many seniors are isolated, especially if they are physically challenged. Your visit may be the highlight of your narrator's day or week; you might be the only person he or she has talked to in several days. If a senior wants to chat over a cup of tea or show you the garden, build this into your schedule and allow enough time. Bring some cookies or flowers.

Everyone appreciates good manners and this is especially true of seniors. Some are likely to treat you as a guest in their homes. Even if they have one room in a nursing home or retirement residence, they will want to ensure your comfort. It's up to you to set the right tone. Graciously accept the niceties, but take enough control that he or she can relax. For example, offer to bring coffee; be the scout and suggest a place for the interview, and when you leave, make sure he or she is comfortable. Replace any furniture or objects you moved to accommodate your interview session.

8.11c The invisible client: The family

If you're contacted (and contracted) by an elderly client, it's understandable that his or her family may wonder who you are, why you're charging what you are, what your credentials are, and if you're on the "up and up." Ask your client if he or she would like you to explain to a family member how you're working together, your terms of payment, the schedule, etc., and if you do get a chance to talk to a family member, ask if there's anything the family thinks you should be aware of.

8.11d Working with frail elderly and hospice patients

Humans, being the complex creatures that we are, means you'll be working in a broad range of circumstances. One of the most difficult is when a client wants to tell their life story but for one reason or another can't do it because of diminished mental agility and/or physical strength. Though we often ruefully wish that people would call us before they or their loved ones began losing control of their faculties, it's likely that you will someday have a client who is frail, ill, or perhaps even facing his or her last days. Others may have physical challenges, chronic pain, or be hearing- or sight-impaired. Some may be losing their memories, be lonely or depressed, and might be unaccustomed to talking about themselves. All these conditions present their own unique challenges. The fact that you can help them is one of the unique rewards of personal history work.

8.11e Working with the critically ill or terminally ill

A person facing a critical illness is sometimes greatly motivated to tell his or her life story. As Linda Blachman, author of *Another Morning: Voices of Truth and Hope from Mothers with Cancer* (California: Seal Press, 2006) puts it, " … critically ill people can summon remarkable focus and energy to complete what is considered an important task of dying: reviewing one's life, harvesting it for meaning, and passing on nuggets of wisdom and messages of love."

My colleague Dan Curtis of Victoria, British Columbia, is a hospice volunteer and has recorded the stories of terminally ill patients. In his blog, www.dancurtis.ca, he makes these points, I print them here with his permission:

- Negotiate how much time your subject feels he or she can handle in any one interview.

- Carefully monitor the strength of your subject while conducting the interview. If you sense he or she is fading, ask if you should stop or continue.

- People at the end of life can't always be at their "charming best." If you find that you're sometimes met with sharpness or even anger, don't take it personally. It's not about you.

- Be calm and mindful with a terminally ill person even if you're not.

- Time is of the essence. Cover the most important topics first. You may not have time to complete the whole story.

- If you can't find a quiet space and must be in a room with others, check with your subject about confidentiality. He or she may feel uncomfortable talking if others can listen in.

- Some medications can make people forgetful, so make sure you know what material you've covered. You may need to remind your subject that he or she has already spoken on a particular topic.

- Your subject may have difficulty hearing. Remember to sit close, no more than three feet away, and to speak clearly and with sufficient volume to be heard.

- Be flexible. Don't be surprised if an interview session you've arranged has to be canceled at the last minute. A terminally ill patient's condition can change dramatically in a short period of time.

- Take care of yourself. Working with someone who is dying is emotionally draining. Make sure you do things that bring you nourishment and strength, such as listening to your favorite music, meditating, doing a vigorous workout, or taking a long relaxing bath.

8.11f Working with the hearing impaired

This may be obvious, but I'll say it anyway: When working with people who can't hear very well, raise your voice and speak clearly. Try to determine early on if they have trouble hearing you. Many people are self-conscious about a hearing loss or the fact that they wear a hearing aid, so it may not be immediately apparent why there seems to be a communication gap. Ask. Simply say, "Can you hear my questions okay?"

8.11g Working with people with dementia/Alzheimer's

Working with a storyteller experiencing the onset of dementia can be one of the most challenging — and rewarding — jobs you'll have. Memory loss is a frightening spectre for both the storyteller and his or her family, and you can do them a great service by capturing the stories and preserving them.

If you're asked to work with a person with signs of dementia or Alzheimer's, meet the person first so you can decide whether or not you'll be able to get any coherent stories. Ask a few sample questions and see what response you get.

If you and the family decide to go ahead, there are some things you should keep in mind.

- Time is of the essence.

- Ask what he or she is proud of and wants people to know, and about his or her favorite memories.

- Look through a photo album and have him or her talk about the people and places.

- Often, earlier memories are more easily retrieved than later ones, so ask about his or her childhood.

- It might be helpful to have a family member present who could offer gentle reminders to the narrator, and help retrieve a word, or give context.

If the narrator is not able to tell the stories, an alternative is to interview his or her family, friends, workmates, neighbors — anyone who could contribute a story or memory about the person's life. With this information and perhaps some quotes from the person himself or herself, you could patch together some lovely tributes.

9
MARKETING

Running your own business is all about marketing yourself. No one is going to ring your doorbell and ask, "Excuse me, do you know anyone I could pay to help me with my family history?" You have to get out there. In this section we'll explore all the facets of marketing, starting with market research.

1. Market Research

1.1 Why you need market research

Market research is what you do to develop an effective marketing strategy. It's crucial to the success of your business. It's not good enough to know that you have a great idea and know that surely there must be a lot of customers who will hire you. You need a plan — an informed plan — on the most effective ways to reach your customers and persuade them to buy what you're offering. There's a reason large companies spend millions of dollars researching their markets: because it works.

Market research provides vital information such as:

- the potential size of your customer base
- who your clients are: where they live; what products they want and why they want them; what will make them buy something in particular; what will make them buy your product and what they're willing to pay for it; how they shop; and how you can best reach them and sell to them

- what your competition is doing
- who your suppliers are
- what market trends will affect your business.

Your findings will help you tailor your products and prices, and help you spend your marketing dollars wisely.

Market research is an ongoing process as you run your business, but there's a lot you should do before you start. It could mean the difference between a long, slow, expensive struggle to find your niche and your customers, or a "hit the ground running" launch.

1.2 Customers

What you want to find out about your customer is not what customers you should be selling to. You should already have decided what you're going to be offerin g (life stories, wedding/romance stories, memoir-writing workshops, business histories, etc.). Market research helps you discover how to reach your target customer by knowing who they are.

You're looking for specifics such as:

- **Geographics:** Where do they live? Will you focus on your town, the region, the country, the world? How big is your potential market?

- **Demographics:** Are your customers likely to be female or male? Are they from large families? What are their income brackets? Occupations? Level of education? Ethnicity? Relationship or parental status?

- **Psychographics:** What do they care about? What affects their buying habits? What kind of advertising do they best respond to? What do they have in common? Where would they look for a service like yours?

1.3 Understanding your competition

What's going to make people hire you instead of your competitor? By knowing your competition, you can design a strategy to be a customer's best choice. What you need to know about your competition is:

- their products: how they price them, and what services they offer;
- who buys their products and services;
- where they advertise;
- length of time in business; and
- any limitations of theirs that you could take advantage of.

Armed with that knowledge, you can strive to offer something superior or unique, whether it's a better price, a better product, your expertise, or exceptional customer service.

You might not have much luck if you call up a local competing company and introduce yourself as someone who would like to take some of their clients away. However, you might be able to gather information from competitors outside your territory with a friendly email asking a few questions, or asking if it would all right for you to call them for a ten-minute chat. Do not call someone expecting a chat without asking over email first, if possible.

Websites are sometimes an excellent source of information. Visit some personal historians' websites and research their products and services, how they market themselves, their brands, who they seem to be selling to, etc.

1.4 SWOT (Strengths, Weaknesses, Opportunities, Threats)

SWOT stands for Strengths, Weaknesses, Opportunities, and Threats. A SWOT analysis of your company helps you see how you can get a competitive advantage over similar companies and develop a stronger business model. When thinking about each SWOT item, you should consider the following:

- **Strengths**: What is your strength? Is it your experience? Your contacts?

- **Weaknesses**: What are your limitations? Inexperience? Lack of funds for equipment or advertising?

- **Opportunities**: What opportunities can you take advantage of? These might be the need for your services, advancements in technology, or the ability to provide superior customer service and a variety of products.

- **Threats**: What are the biggest threats to your business? Write down your worst-case scenarios. Think also about direct competition and indirect competition. Indirect competition includes people not choosing to hire *any* personal historian: people who think they can do their own personal histories, who don't understand the value of a personal history, or who procrastinate until it's too late.

1.5 Suppliers

For a personal history business, your suppliers are likely to be design services, editorial services, transcribers, book printers and binders, places where you'll buy CDs and office supplies, etc. Do some research on their availability and cost.

Try calling or emailing some of your potential suppliers and asking them about their customers. You might be surprised at how knowledgeable they are about what's going on in the field of memoirs and family histories. For instance, a bookbinder might reveal that just last month he bound seven memoir books!

1.6 Market trends

What market are you stepping into, or do you hope to create? What could affect your business? Do you live in an area with a large number of retirees? Is your town experiencing an economic crisis such as a factory closure? If so, where do you need to go to make sales, or how could you adjust your prices to reach a larger number of people? What's in the newspapers and magazines? We know there's a huge interest in family stories and memoirs, so read everything you can about how the industry is developing. Also follow trends and developments in technology. Anything that is directly or peripherally involved in your business should be on your radar screen.

1.7 Primary and secondary resources

Your market research should come from a variety of sources, both primary (information you gather straight from the source, such as from your potential customers or your competition or suppliers), and secondary (information gathered from other sources such as the Internet, newspapers, etc.).

1.8 Primary research: A customer survey

Go straight to the horse's mouth, so to speak, and do a customer survey. Conduct a survey either in person, over the phone, via email, or by an online service such as Survey Monkey or Boomerang. Start by writing down the names of at least 50 people. Include people you know and people you don't know. For the latter, ask friends and family for the names of two or three people they think would not mind being contacted by you. Try your connections on LinkedIn, Facebook, or Twitter. Members of a networking group would also be good sources, as would any professionals in your life, such as a doctor, dentist, accountant, lawyer, or hairstylist. Your survey shouldn't be long. It should take someone no longer than about seven minutes to complete. A survey is not the place or time to solicit business; if it sounds like a sales pitch, people will not provide you with the information you want.

Two of the most popular types of questionnaires are:

- a list of possible answers ("How much would you be willing to spend to have your memoirs recorded and preserved in a book?"), and

- a rating or ranking scale ("On a scale of 1 to 10 with 10 being the highest, how important is it to you to save your family's stories?")

Decide what you need to know about your market, then test some questions on a family member or friend. Some information you might want to gather includes:

- the age of the respondent

- the extent of his or her interest in a personal memoir or family history

- whether he or she would want to somehow preserve his or her life story or that of an older family member

- if not, why not

- if he or she would pay someone to help

- how much he or she would be willing to pay

- what his or her preferred end product is

- what qualities he or she would look for in a personal biographer or family historian

You could also ask for general comments and allow people to indicate whether they'd like you to let them know when you launch your business. Assure your respondents that their information will be held strictly confidential and you will not contact them again unless they've asked you to. If they do respond (and you can probably count on a 30 percent survey return), be sure to thank them.

1.9 Sources of secondary research

The Internet makes secondary research easier than poring over stacks at the library, but you'll still need to do a lot of digging either way. Check out these sources:

- Government: All levels of government (federal, state or provincial, and local) are great sources for statistics about residents and businesses.

- Business directories, both in print and online

- Libraries

- Online directories such as those available through Yahoo! and Google

- Boards of trade and chambers of commerce

- Small-business centers

2. Marketing Your Business

You can have the best service and product in the world, but if no one knows about these, you may as well pull up a rocking chair and turn on the TV. You have to get out there.

Don't be intimidated by marketing. You already know a lot about it because you're constantly bombarded with marketing messages. What kinds of marketing do you respond to? What influences your own buying decisions? Analyzing what works for you is a great start to putting together a strategy.

If you believe in yourself and your business, all you have to do is tell people about it. Simple as that sounds, it's true. The days of the hard sell are over. Consumers are much more savvy than they used to be. They educate themselves, do a lot of Internet research before they buy, and they demand respect for their knowledge, education, experience, and age. If you are properly prepared with information, experience, and the right product at the right price at the right time, customers will want to do business with you. But you still have to go out and find them.

2.1 Your message

2.1a Sell the benefits

Which has more impact? Benefits like, "You'll hear your grandma's voice telling your family's favorite stories. It will be just like she's in the room with you again," or features such as "We use lavaliere microphones and sophisticated audio editing software." Pretty obvious, isn't it?

Examine some marketing materials and effective advertising campaigns. You'll see that the best ones emphasize the benefits and value to the customer — not the features. In all your marketing efforts, whether written or spoken, remember that it's not about what you do, it's about what you can do for your customers. Good marketing is telling your customers what owning your product will mean to them, and how it can improve their lives. For instance, your product may be CDs or books, but what you're really selling is a family legacy and stronger intergenerational bonds as well as peace of mind, satisfaction, and relief. People don't care how sharp the photographs are going to be. They care about what a personal or family history will do for their parents, for themselves, and for their children. They care about being able to wipe that big, very important task off

their huge list of things to do, knowing that a professional is going to handle everything, start to finish.

2.1b Be your authentic self

Whether you're writing website copy or speaking to a group, you must first believe in what you're selling. If you're passionate about it, your enthusiasm will be contagious and people will want to listen. People can see through hollow sales talk, so don't try to sound like something you're not. Be yourself, and practice different ways of talking and writing about what you do until it feels right.

2.2 Your marketing plan

A marketing plan is a written policy of your marketing strategy. Like a business plan, your marketing plan will be an organic thing that grows and changes as your business takes shape. In it, you'll chart out what you're going to do, when you're going to do it, and how much it will cost.

Ideally, your marketing plan will include:

- A description of your business: what you do and how you do it.

- Plans for expansion and additional products.

- Your target market: What you learned from your market research such as the who, where and why of your ideal client.

- Sales forecasts: How much do you plan to sell? Be specific. For instance, "I plan to sell one oral history every month for the first nine months of business and two personal history books in the first year."

- Marketing strategy: Marketing strategy takes into account the 5 Ps of marketing — Product, Price, Place, Promotion, and Packaging. Or remember this old adage:

A successful business relies on offering the right product, at the right place, at the right time. Your marketing strategy identifies what you're offering (Product — including the benefits of your product — and Packaging), how much it's going to cost (Price), and how and where you're going to sell it (Promotion and Place).

As you're writing your marketing strategy, answer the following questions:

- How will you communicate with your target market?

- What are your strengths? (e.g., establish yourself as the go-to person for personal history services in your town and how you will accomplish this.)

- How will you generate interest in your business?

- How will you create a desire to purchase your product or service?

- What strategic alliances will you make? For instance, if you are doing house histories, do you have contacts in the real estate profession?

- Products and services (including your pricing strategy): What are you offering, and what will you charge for each product or service? Explain the rationale behind your decisions.

- Promotion and publicity plans: How do you plan on promoting your business?

- Your marketing budget

  - How much can you spend on marketing materials such as a website, business cards, and brochures?

  - Do you plan to advertise? Where? How much will it cost?

- Don't forget those occasional marketing expenses such as renting a booth at a trade show or business fair. Signage is expensive. A banner alone can cost $300 and up.

- Marketing action plan: List specific tasks and goals, when you will complete them, and what the objectives are.

Sample 16 is a marketing plan template. It is also available on the CD-ROM. Use it to think through each marketing issue for your business.

2.3 Marketing to the 50+ demographic

Generally speaking, your target market is likely people over 50 who wish to preserve their life stories, family histories, or the stories of their parents or grandparents. There are, of course, many exceptions but I think it's fair to say that most of your clients will be what society considers "older."

Ten years ago, anyone over the age of 50 got lumped into a demographic called "the senior market," but today, savvy marketers are realizing that this market segment is actually widely diversified in buying habits, interests, values, etc. Of course it is: It has an age span of at least 40 years!

One size does not fit all in today's older market, and this is very true in the personal history business. It is quite common to first be contacted by a baby boomer, someone in his or her 50s or 60s, who wants to capture the stories of a parent or grandparent. Often, they're the ones paying for the service. But they may not be. They may be just checking you out to make sure their parents don't get overcharged, or to make sure you're the kind of person their parents would like — *then* they'll approach their parents with the

MARKETING PLAN TEMPLATE

Mary Jane Memoirs

(Term covered in this plan; e.g., First Six Months of Operation)

Description of Business

(Describe what you do and how you do it, as well as plans for future offerings. Think back to your business plan described in Sample 1.)

Target Market

(Who is your ideal client? Where does he or she live? What makes him or her your target client?)

Sales Forecasts

(How much do you plan to sell, and when?)

Marketing Strategy

(In this section, describe your products and services. How will you price your products and services? What benefits do you offer your customers? Also write about any packaging that may apply, your promotional and publicity plans, and any strategic alliances you may form with other like-minded businesses and how you will accomplish them. Finally, discuss your marketing budget and how much you will allocate to marketing materials, advertising, etc.)

Marketing Action Plan

(Explain what you'll be doing, when, where, and how.)

idea to do their personal histories, and have the parents pay for it. You may have to "sell" yourself all over again to the parent.

Because of this "double-edged" market, you need to have different approaches: one that appeals to the adult child in his or her late 40s, 50s, or early 60s, and one that appeals to the parent in his or her late 60s, 70s, 80s, or 90s. Even within those two groups there are many differences. An "active retiree" age, say, 62 to mid-70s, is a different market than the older senior in his or her late 70s, 80s, or 90s.

2.3a Baby boomers versus active retirees and seniors

I'm indebted to Kurt Medina, co-author of *77 Truths About Marketing to the 50+ Consumer* for parts of the following list of characteristics. The rest is what I've found through general research and my own observations.

Baby boomers, (currently) approximately aged 47 to 65, generally share these characteristics:

- Have built some wealth but are still very price conscious, probably a result of being raised by Depression-era parents.

- Busy and time-stressed: may be caring for their parents and raising a family (and may have their own adult children living at home); probably working at least part-time.

- Are willing to try something new just because it is new. This is the generation that saw TV come into their living rooms, and the invention of the computer and the Internet.

- Want to take an educated, proactive role in buying decisions; likely to do their own investigation and research prior to contacting you. Having choices will

appeal to their desire to have control over their spending.

- Skeptical of hype. Prefer simple, honest messages.

- Feel a sense of entitlement because that's the way it's always been: They are a generation accustomed to opportunity, affluence, optimism, and instant gratification.

- Appreciate efficiency and convenience.

- Are more concerned about the welfare of their parents than any previous generation.

- Want products that add to their life experience.

Active retirees and seniors generally share these characteristics:

- More likely to buy because of perceived value for money. Many of this age group lived through the Depression and still feel money is something that should be saved, not spent.

- Do not like surprises. "Deliver what's promised and what's expected," and make sure those two things are in alignment.

- Will try something new if they can see it actually benefiting them.

- Seniors are more likely to read direct mail and print marketing materials; active retirees are more likely to use the Internet and email.

- Respond to positive images of real people doing what they're doing: being active and healthy, enjoying life.

- Some may feel a sense of entitlement by virtue of living a long life, enduring some hardship, but the entitlement is more about being respected and having earned the right to do and say whatever they want.

- Seniors relate better to boomers and people their own age.

Seniors appreciate superior customer service, politeness, extras, giveaways, and service people who don't watch the clock and are willing to pass the time of day with them.

2.4 Marketing materials

Anything that helps you sell your products or services is under the umbrella of marketing materials.

2.4a The big one: Your business card

A business card is absolutely necessary. Always keep a bunch with you. If someone wants to buy you a nice little gift to help launch your business, tell him or her that a classy-looking business card holder would be very welcome.

Ever get handed a business card and can't figure out what the business is? Boring business cards are one thing, but it's another to make them indecipherable by trying to cram so much information onto them that you can't read the print, your eye is searching for the name of the business or the person's name, or the information just makes no sense. If your business name is Mary Jane Memoirs, it's pretty obvious what you do, but if your business name is Memories by Mary Jane, that could be interpreted a number of ways. That's where a business card comes in. It helps to say exactly what the business is about, who you are in the business, and how people can contact you or get more information. Keep it simple with lots of white space.

For the first few months you're in business, I think a standard, inexpensive card is fine.

This is the time when you'll be defining your image so you shouldn't spend a big whack of money on fancy business cards, only to change your logo in six months and find you have 940 rectangles of heavy white paper that you can't bear to throw away just yet because they cost you good money. By "standard" I mean all you need is your name, your business name and tagline (the phrase that ties in with your business name, as explained in Chapter 4), your contact information, and your website if you have one.

Once you establish your look, with a logo, colors, etc., invest in some good quality cards. If you're reasonably computer savvy you could do them yourself using a template from an online company or a print shop. If you're lucky, you'll find a helpful employee who can just tweak your design. If you have custom colors, you will definitely want to see a proof copy before you get your cards printed. Colors that look wonderful on a computer monitor can look dreadful — or at least different — in print.

Tip: If you've paid a designer to create a logo for you, you might be able to get him or her to design your business cards for an extra small fee.

What makes a great business card?

1. It should reflect you. Give it some personality!

2. Think of your target audience. If you're going to be producing engagement/wedding books, a flowing, romantic script would be a lot better than something heavy and stodgy.

3. Use graphics sparingly. Images (including your photo if you choose) should blend with the text in your overall message; they should be eye-catching

but not so prominent that they distract from the information on the card.

4. Should you put your photo on your card? I lean toward no, but some experts think it's a good thing to do if you're in a personal service industry like ours. My own preference is to use the limited space on a business card to convey information.

5. Contact information. Your email address should, ideally, be integrated with your website, e.g., jcampbell@ heritagememoirs.ca, not the email address you have through your Internet Service Provider (ISP). That way you eliminate any worry about having to change email addresses when you change ISPs, and it looks much more business-like. Many people do not put their street address on their business card, the rationale being that it's unnecessary and may in fact deter people from contacting you if they feel you live too far away. Plus, if you move, you have to have new cards printed.

6. Consider using the back of the card for additional information, a special offer, an inspirational quote, or a simple graphic in your special color.

7. Go with the standard size, not something you think will stand out because it's oversized or an odd shape. You want people to keep your card and that means being able to store it along with their other cards.

8. Consider your card in fridge-magnet format. Hiring a personal historian is usually not a snap decision. Most people seem to think about it for months, if not years, before taking action to do their memoirs or preserve their family's stories. So for our purposes, a fridge magnet

business card may be a very good way to remind people and keep our names front and center.

9. A quality card says you offer a quality product.

A final word about business cards: Give them away. Lots of them. They're a cheap and effective marketing tool but not if they stay in your purse or pocket.

2.4b Custom-printed stationery

Stationery with your logo, name, and address adds a professional touch to invoices, sales letters, and press releases and can be very affordable. In fact, if you have a color printer you can print your own.

2.4c Brochures

Brochures used to be important, but now the Internet makes it easy for anyone to have a multimedia, interactive, colorful, ever-changing brochure called a website. However, it's impressive and professional to leave something tangible like an informative brochure in people's hands, especially if the hands belong to a serious potential client. But for handing out at a trade show or, heaven forbid, leaving in a library or community center, a brochure might not be worth the money. Anything decent-looking will have to be professionally designed and printed on quality paper, and this is not cheap. For every ten you give out, eight will probably get thrown in the garbage after a fleeting glance. One might hang around on someone's kitchen table for a few weeks or months and then get thrown away. However, the other might just lead to a contract one day.

2.4d Postcard

I love getting snail mail addressed to me — it's almost a novelty now. A postcard can be a great marketing tool; bigger than a business card, cheaper than a brochure, and delivered straight to a potential client's door. You can put a photo of your products on the front, or some other attractive graphic, and use the back to advertise a special offer, or just outline your services. It's best if you have something "newsy" as an excuse to send one, but it's not absolutely necessary. Send one to everyone on your contact list. It's relatively easy to design a postcard, too; you can find templates online or in some productivity suites such as iWork. You'll spend money on postage, but as a business you'll likely get a discount on bulk mailings from the post office.

2.4e Samples/presentation folder/ media kit

Many interested prospects, especially the elderly, prefer printed materials over websites.

A presentation folder with your business name and logo printed on the front will do the trick. Inside, have your business card, a one-page summary of your products and services with price ranges, a general article about personal history such as one on the importance of telling your life story, and some information about you — just a couple of paragraphs about your background, your business, projects you've worked on, accomplishments, and the like. This page can also have client testimonials. If you've had some press coverage, include reprints of the articles (after securing copyright or permission to reprint).

This presentation folder can also serve as a kit that you can send to various media. For this purpose I would definitely include a photo and bio, and perhaps a question-and-answer sheet that provides more promotional-type information than you'd give a customer. For instance, you want to convey to the media why they (i.e., their readers) should be interested in your business and you, whereas for a customer, you want to convey what your business can do for them. If possible, your media kit should include statistics, survey results, some facts and figures — something current and newsworthy.

2.4f Business video

A three- to five-minute video that showcases you and your business is your multimedia business card. It can go on your website and on a CD that you leave with clients. You could show yourself with a client and talk about the importance of telling your life story, show some of your products, and talk about how they're made.

10
YOUR ONLINE PRESENCE

1. Your Website

If you're not on the Internet, you could be missing out on 90 percent of your business opportunities. Blogs, e-newsletters, and social media can be important lead-generators, plus they all support your main effort: your website. In this chapter I'll outline why you need to be online and what you can do to make your website shine. Then we'll look at a few other sites, services, and networks you can use to build awareness of your online presence.

1.1 Do you really need a website?

If you had just one marketing item on your agenda for the first three months of your business (not likely!), I would advise you make it your website. People of all ages and walks of life turn to the Internet to browse through the marketplace, checking products, services, prices, reputation, qualifications, information, and of course figuring out how to find you. You can be sure your potential clients are reading your competition's websites, so be sure they're reading yours, too. If you don't have a website, many people will question your credibility and level of professionalism.

1.2 Do it now

Even if it's just a temporary, one-page site, put something up that tells people what you do and who you are. It's okay to post a message that your new site will be coming soon, but don't wait too long to get it up and running. You might even offer to alert visitors when your new site is launched. Even better, give them an incentive to share their email address with you, like something free or a discount on services.

Don't get caught in analysis paralysis. If you're a perfectionist (or is that procrastinator?) like me you will research and analyze and edit something until it's lying on the ground begging for mercy. Just do it. It doesn't matter if it's not perfect. Write some copy, or allow someone else to do it for you, and wish it godspeed as it enters cyberspace.

Tip: Please do not lift copy from other personal historians' (or anyone's) websites. It's unethical and the copy will sound false. Be original.

1.3 Do it yourself or hire a pro?

Design and content really go hand-in-hand, and if one is weak it makes the other one weak. Unless you're a designer, I strongly recommend you hire somebody to design your website. Just like your business card and logo, the quality of your website speaks volumes about the quality of your work.

It may well be worth your while to also hire a writer to create your content, even if you are a writer. Writing for the Web is a special skill. A professional writer can work with you so that your website conveys your message in the most effective, engaging way.

Don't skimp on your website. Most people need help in both design and content and you probably will, too. As always, shop around, look closely at portfolios, and talk to the person and listen for an exceptional level of expertise and professionalism. Ask for references, and know exactly what you're paying for.

1.4 Domain name

Your website has a unique domain name, which is your Internet address or Universal Resource Locator (URL). Securing a domain name is the first step in developing a website. Google "domain name" or "domain name registration" for a list of companies that show you how to register a domain name.

As mentioned in Chapter 4, it's great if you can secure a domain name that's the same as your business name, but this might be impossible. You might have to go with an edited version, such as with hyphens (www.mary-jane-memoirs.com) or an add-on (www.maryjanememoirsbusiness.com). And if you do find an available domain name that you like, grab it immediately. Even if you're not 100 percent sure that you'll keep it, it's cheap insurance. Long before I got my first client or had a clue what I was doing, I registered www.personalhistories.ca. In addition to www.heritagememoirs.ca, I have a few others that I'll probably never use — but they seemed like a good idea at the time! You can always redirect these extra URLs to your main website.

1.5 Web hosting

Once you have your site designed, you need to put it on the World Wide Web through a web hosting company. You can upload your own files if you wish, or have your designer do it. Some web hosting companies are full service, in that they will do everything from registering your domain name, designing your site, to hosting it for one flat fee per month. If you want to change something, you just email them and they will take care of it. No worries about learning HTML or FTPing your changes to your web hosting company.

1.6 Navigation/general

Remember that your visitors are one click away from leaving your site, and if they've had a disappointing visit, they won't return. You have one chance to impress them and keep them there long enough to meet your goals. Keeping people engaged and on your site is called "stickiness."

So, what are the goals you wish to accomplish with your website?

Your website's primary goal should be to get people so intrigued and excited that they'll contact you for more information. You're probably not going to make a sale by your website alone. You want to talk to the visitors or email them and establish a relationship. That's the first step toward gaining new customers.

For this reason, it's best not to have too much information on your site. Give visitors enough that they understand what it is you do; enough that they can figure out if this is what they want. Focus. Don't make people hunt for the information they want. Tell them what you do, why they'd want to hire you, how it all works, and at least a range of how much it costs. If you give people too many options or make the rest of the content too hard to find, they'll go straight to your "prices" page, and you want to avoid that.

1.7 Value-added content

Having said that you shouldn't go into too much detail, the more truly informative and useful content you have on your site, the more interesting it is. Think about why and how people would find your site through a search engine (as opposed to already knowing and typing in your URL). What are they looking for? Chances are, they're interested in family history, memoirs, life stories, writers, publishers, or whatever your focus is. They may not be looking specifically to hire someone; they just want information. Tell them why they should preserve their stories, and in what ways they can do that. Sure, tell them about your services, but also provide some good, free information about getting started; maybe an Articles section where you've written a series about the health benefits of life review, or "Top 10 Tips for Interviewing Relatives." For every visitor who learns enough from your information to actually do it themselves, there could be 500 who have stayed on your site and found out more about your business and who will consider getting some help with their project. Guess who they're going to call? You, because you've shown them some of your expertise in the personal history field; you've given something to them, free, that they can use; you've shown them you can write intelligently.

Another reason to have great content is so that other sites will link to you as a good information source, which will help get you a higher ranking in search engines such as Google.

1.8 Sections of your website

There's good reason why most business websites follow the model, or variations of, "Home," "About," "Products and Services," "Pricing and Process," " Testimonials," "In the News," and "Contact Us" pages. These are now recognized terms and get people where they want to go. You don't have to follow this model, of course. You can be as creative as you wish.

1.8a Home page

Your home page, also known as the index page, is where people who type in your URL will land first. Things to remember about this main page:

- Make it quick to load. If you use Flash (the animation application for the Web), spinning globes, and sound, or have a lot of images or they're not formatted properly by the web programmer, the page will load painfully slowly. If your visitor's kettle is boiling or the phone is ringing, he or she is just as likely to impatiently close the browser window without even seeing your site.

- The goal of your home page is to draw people further into your site. It should provide a clear idea of what you do and what they'll find on your site. Or better yet, why they should even care to explore it.

- Visitors should immediately see how they can contact you.

- Realize that people don't read websites; they scan. There are lots of books and resources that will help you write effective copy for the Web, but in general, your copy should be in manageable bites, not a long buffet. Use headings to tell visitors what that paragraph or section is about, so you're not wasting their time making them read irrelevant content.

- Make liberal use of keywords that the search engines are looking for. Google, Yahoo!, and the other search engines send out robots looking for sites with the most relevance to the terms people are searching for. Put yourself in the shoes of your typical customer. What words or phrases would you use if you were looking for a service like yours? Make sure you have lots of these keywords in your content.

- Besides the navigation menu, try to include links within your copy. For instance, if you have a page called "Process," you'll have "Process" on your navigation menu. But in addition, you can give it some context in your copy on the other pages, such as "With every personal history project,

we take care to make the process as enjoyable as possible." The word "process" can be linked to the Process page.

1.8b About

This is the place to toot your horn. Tell people a bit about yourself. If you're just starting out, you can't talk too much about your personal history experience, but you can talk about prior experience that makes you qualified. Highlight your experience interviewing, writing, or editing; your design work for a publication; your experience working with the elderly or in a counselling role; your expertise in photo restoration or organizing, etc. Talk about how you got into the personal history business and why, but keep it relatively brief.

If it applies, talk about presentations you've given (where and when), media coverage (link to your In the News page), awards, and education and training.

1.8c Pricing

To post your prices or not post your prices — that's your big question. There are pros and cons for both sides.

Posting your prices makes your position in the marketplace very clear; are you no-frills, standard, or high-end? If you've priced yourself well and fairly, I don't see any reason not to post your prices. Your visitors can check out what you charge and decide to contact you or not; it's simple. If you don't post your prices, you'll get calls from people who have no idea what a personal history costs. You could spend an hour or so talking with them before you both determine that their budget is far too low to be able to afford your services. If you do post your prices, your conversations can focus on what you can do for the prospect, and not be clouded by the big mystery of how much it's going to cost. You're pre-qualifying customers who have the budget to buy your services, which seems to me a smart marketing strategy.

Some personal historians don't want to publish their prices because their competitors will see what they charge. But, what's wrong with having your competitors know what you charge? If they want to price themselves lower than you, let them. You know what you want (or need) to charge in order to make this business viable. Besides, this is not a business where people hire someone based solely on price. Some business people state right up front, "If you're looking for the cheapest product, I'm not it. I'm also not the most expensive."

However, by posting your prices you might be turning away customers who immediately balk. They won't even allow their initial excitement to percolate because they're thinking "Well, forget that. There's no way I can afford that." I don't really buy this argument either, though. If they get sticker shock to the point where they decide against a project, I'd rather they get sticker shock while they're reading my website, not after I've spent an hour on the phone or composing an email with a customized project proposal.

In general, I believe consumers prefer to see published prices. I think if you're not upfront, you run the risk of people thinking that your custom quote will be whatever you think the market will bear — in other words, it's flexible — and that can mean it's flexible UPward, too. Prices right there in black and white tell them your prices are tried and true, that you've thought them out, and that others have paid the same amount.

Consumers are doing due diligence on the Internet as they shop for everything from mattresses to batteries to retirement homes. Today's baby boomers are well educated when

it comes to shopping online and they are busy, which means they appreciate having all the information at their fingertips. For this reason, I think it's wise to save them time whenever we can.

1.8d Client testimonials

Once you've done a few projects, you'll be able to post all kinds of accolades and testaments to your stellar work from satisfied customers. Until then, try to get some quotes from people you've worked with, even if they just speak to your writing ability, project management skills, or whatever your focus is.

1.8e Samples

It's worth it to get some great photos of your books, quilts, attractively packaged audio CDs, etc. People want to see the finished product. Some personal historians show a sample of how a raw transcript is edited into a flowing narrative — a before-and after-scenario.

1.8f Contact

You can put your contact information at the bottom of every page if you wish, but you'll also want a dedicated contact page. Whether you post your mailing address is up to you. Since telephones and the Internet make it possible to do business anywhere in the world, you might just want to provide your email address and telephone number. However, if you plan to do most of your business close to home, it's a good idea to include your mailing address. I think a lot of people feel more comfortable knowing where the place of business is; that it's a real, live person that they're dealing with. If you're concerned that people won't contact you if you live in a remote area, state that your service area includes a much wider radius and name specific cities and regions.

If you have a preference for how you want people to contact you, state this on your site. Most people are comfortable with email now, or filling out a contact form, but there is another group that will just want to pick up the phone. I think it's a good idea, in light of all the spam and junk we get, to assure people that their email addresses are strictly confidential and they won't be contacted without their consent.

A final word about your contact page. If you state that you will respond to an email or phone inquiry within a certain length of time — 24 hours, two business days, whatever you choose — make sure you do.

1.8g In the news

If you're lucky enough to get media coverage, be sure to include it on your website. Nothing is quite so impressive as being featured in a newspaper or magazine article or talking on TV or radio about your business.

Beware of copyright issues. You are usually not allowed to post a published article, or even a link to the media outlet's website where the article is archived, without permission and usually a hefty fee. Most web hosting companies won't violate copyright regulations, and rightly so. Even if your website hosting company will bend the rules, it speaks badly of your professional ethics. Think of a reporter who's interested in writing a feature about you seeing a PDF of another article on your site, one for which you do not have permission to post. Is he or she going to be in a hurry to interview you so you can do the same to them? Small, local papers may be happy to give you permission without a fee. When in doubt, ask. If it's too expensive, you can usually post short excerpts, or at least mention the coverage and link to it. Even the fact that you've been featured in a newspaper or magazine speaks to your reputation.

If you've been on TV, radio, or in a podcast, you could post a clip on your site provided you get permission. Use your website to its fullest multimedia capability.

1.9 Look and feel

What image do you want to convey? Your website is a vital part of your brand and should complement every other marketing piece, from your business card to your stationery. It should certainly have your logo prominently displayed.

Design-wise, keep it simple. I like web eye-candy as much as the next person, and maybe I'm a little biased because I'm a writer, but there's a lot of truth to the statement "content is king." I believe form should follow function. I've seen gorgeous-looking sites that don't tell you where to go next, what the company is, or even what's clickable. I've also seen fairly dull-looking sites that have great content that I return to again and again.

2. Writing for a Personal History Website

Well-crafted copy can grab people's attention, touch their hearts, establish your credibility, build trust, spur people into taking action, involve them in the project, help them visualize the final product, interest them, and educate them. They've come to your site because they probably already have a project in mind, so unless you somehow manage to throw a wet blanket onto their hopes and dreams, all you have to do is feed their excitement.

The best websites are a good balance of information and self-promotion. There's no faster way to drive people away than slick sales talk. Avoid copy that sounds like a hard sell or which has a desperate tone, like "Call me right now!"

Website DON'Ts:

- Little icons such as mailboxes that open and close

- Automatic sounds. Ever go to a website and immediately get bombarded with "O Sole Mio" or a disembodied voice? I hate that. Give people the choice whether they want sound.

- Visitor counters. Ho hum. Who cares if he or she is the 345th visitor?

- Pop-up (or under) windows of any kind.

- Animated fingers going back and forth to indicate where you should click next.

- Background graphics that are so heavy you can't read the text.

- Pages that are so long they're just a sea of words, and long pages that don't have "back to top" links.

- No indication of how to return to the previous page.

- Content that is merely sales talk and doesn't answer the needs of visitors.

Website DOs:

- Chunks of information in short paragraphs with descriptive titles

- Value-added material such as articles and links to useful sites

- "Rewards" for visiting the site, such as giveaways

- Ways to capture email addresses, such as an offer to send visitors something free in exchange for signing up for a newsletter

- Regular updates that make visitors want to return to see what's new

- Clear navigation, back and forth

- Good balance of space and text/graphics

- Free of typos, errors and broken links

- Most if not all content is "above the fold." This term originally and still does refer to a newspaper being folded in half to fit a newsstand. Buyers only see the content above the fold so this is where the editor would place the biggest news of the day. Where possible, keep your most important content immediately prominent and visible and don't make your visitors scroll down.

3. Search Engine Optimization (SEO)

You want your website to be as busy as Grand Central Station, preferably with people who are buying tickets and boarding the train. Your goal is to maximize both the quantity and quality of your traffic; you want lots and lots of visitors, and visitors who intend to be there and didn't just land there by accident.

Search Engine Optimization (SEO) is the process of giving your site the best chance of ranking highly in search engine results, which of course leads to more visitors who are looking for your type of business. When a user enters keywords into a search engine like Google or Yahoo!, the sites that appear near the top of the results list have been deemed the most relevant to those keywords. SEO is now so important and complex that entire companies are devoted to it. SEO takes time and knowledge and you will therefore pay handsomely if you don't want to do it yourself. But you can do a lot yourself.

I encourage you to research SEO best practices, and when you're looking for a web designer and/or hosting firm, ask good questions about what help they offer for SEO. Any good firm should at least tell you what you as the creator can do, and what they do on their programming and formatting end. Here are just a few tips to keep in mind:

- As mentioned, keywords are vitally important to getting your site noticed by the search engines.

- Try to get other sites to link to you because this helps improve your ranking. One way to do this is to provide objective, informative content on your site that other sites might want to link to. Another is to do reciprocal links with colleagues and alliances, and to get your site listed in business directories.

- Keep your content updated. Post informative newsy items about the personal history world.

- Make sure your web designer is knowledgeable about meta tags and especially about the titles of pages.

4. Other Tips

4.1 Your email signature

Create an email signature and use it whenever you're communicating with anyone remotely connected with your business. It might include your full name, business name, telephone number, website address (URL), and your tagline. Don't make it too long. I've seen signatures that are eight or nine lines, with everything from inspirational quotes to announcements of upcoming presentations.

4.2 Website or blog?

Blogs can be a very effective alternative to a website. In fact, they can be websites themselves. They are easy to create, inexpensive or free, can be quickly updated, and are search-engine friendly — they have a lot of content and constantly refreshed material. Blogs can add a personal touch and help to build a relationship with your visitors. As people read your blog they will get to know you and trust you, and in business, that's a good thing. The writing can be a little more casual than that of a business's website. And they can be interactive: Visitors can post comments and you can respond. You can use a blog to write your views about events, articles, or issues, which adds to your authority; and write reviews about websites or products that your visitors might be interested in, such as software that creates a family tree.

The disadvantage of a blog is that you have to keep it updated with compelling content. If you have the skills and the time, that's fine, but don't start one unless you're willing to dedicate several hours per week.

It doesn't have to an "either/or" situation. Blogs can be integrated into your website and your web hosting firm or designer can tell you how to do this. Whether they're stand-alone or integrated, they give you lots of opportunities to link to your website and tell your visitors how to connect with you through the social media sites described in section **4.3**.

4.3 Social media: LinkedIn/ Facebook/Twitter/Eons/ MySpace/YouTube

When Tim Berners-Lee proposed the World Wide Web around 1989, he was building on his initial concept of facilitating the sharing of up-to-date information among researchers. Today, user-generated content through social media sites is changing the face of how we communicate and how we do business — and is itself changing at such a rapid pace that anything I write here may well be outdated by the time you read this book.

Entrepreneurs use social media sites like Facebook, LinkedIn, and Twitter to build buzz around their businesses and to get people telling other people about their services. That, in turn, helps build their brand (get it recognized) and build a database of contacts. Business owners can also share information and resources through online communities, become known as experts in their field, and build loyalty. The possible numbers of people discovering your business is staggering, people who would otherwise never hear about you, and best of all — it's free!

Some experts in marketing to the 50+ age demographic say social media is not the best way to market your services — at least, it's not the best way to spend your time. Surveys show that 90 percent of people 55 and older who are online are using it for email and the percentage using it for social media is around 10 percent. But why dismiss it and risk losing out on potential buyers? Anything that helps increase your presence on the Web is worthwhile.

Why not try it? Do some research, and experiment with different services. It only takes a few minutes to compose a profile on LinkedIn or Facebook, for instance, and you never know who's going to view your information. For more concentrated efforts, there are companies that specialize in "Internet presence management" — helping you make the most of online opportunities, which are increasing every day.

4.4 E-newsletter/e-zine

An informative, entertaining newsletter with tips about life-story writing, or whatever your focus is, is another great way to stay connected with your customer base. You create it, send it to your contacts, and it appears as an email in their inbox. Sure, some will be fast with the "delete" key, but some people will look forward to your mailing. Some of your topics could include:

- Tips on how to create a family newsletter.
- Tips on how to capture memories of kids/babies' first five years.
- Software programs that help organize digital photos.

Here are some things to keep in mind if you do an e-newsletter:

- Start right: Get permission. It's best to have an explicit "opt-in" whereby people on your contact list can specifically agree to receive your e-newsletter, though you could send your first one to everyone and see what the fall-out is. That's forgivable. But ask if they want to continue to receive it, and make it easy for them to unsubscribe.

- Privacy policy: Document your privacy policy and assure your readers that you will never use their email address for any other purpose, you won't share it with anyone, and you'll remove it from your list if they want.

- Keep it brief and interesting: Respect people's time. If you have a longer article posted on your website or blog, provide a link to it in your newsletter.

- Include a personal message: This is a great chance to build a relationship with your readers. For that reason, invite feedback.

- Your goal with a newsletter is to get people to hire you, eventually. Be subtle, but be sure they know what your business is all about.

- Reward loyal readers with discounts and special offers.

- Step out of the box. Expand your sphere. Write about an extension of the personal history field. How about an article about how to throw a book-signing party? Or a review of a newly-published celebrity memoir?

- Provide your readers with an easy way to send their friends either your whole newsletter or just one article. This is called viral marketing because you can spread your marketing message like a virus, from one personal contact to another, and another, and another.

- Begin as you mean to go on: Don't start a newsletter if you can't deliver it regularly. Be realistic about your time commitment.

- Make liberal use of anecdotes, case studies, and useful and timely information. Don't use it to try to sell something. Use it to show your contacts that you care about them, that you've prepared this newsletter specifically for them, free of charge. Of course you'll probably want to mention that terrific press coverage you've received, or how you helped a family reunite, or how your skills made a big difference to a volunteer project ...

- Remember to include at least two links to your website.

- Be sure to give people an easy way to unsubscribe. The last thing you want is to annoy people with an unwanted mailing.

You can find templates for newsletters in Microsoft Office, Mac iWork, and other software programs, and there are many companies that streamline the email newsletter process for you, such as Constant Contact or iContact. Some have nifty features that will help you target your emails and make them more useful to readers, such as the ability to analyze who's opening your email, who's clicking on which links, what the clickthrough rate is, and more.

11
PUBLICITY, PROMOTION, AND REACHING YOUR CLIENTS

From your market research, you know who your ideal clients are. Now you have to figure out how to reach them. You'll spend a good amount of time (and money) on your marketing efforts as described in Chapter 9, so it's wise to really know your area of focus, what works, and what's a waste of time. The possibilities of promotional activities are exciting. In this chapter I offer a few suggestions.

1. The Best Things in Publicity Are Free: Getting Covered in Newspapers, Magazines, and on Radio and TV

Being featured in a newspaper, magazine, or newsletter, or being interviewed on television or radio is the best way to publicize your business. It gives you credibility as a professional, establishes your authority on a subject, and builds your reputation. No amount of advertising dollars can buy this kind of publicity. When it comes from a respected, objective outlet with no vested interest in selling anything, consumers are far more likely to believe that it's true.

1.1 Know your angle

The media is hungry for news and features about interesting events, people, stories, products and services, trends, tips, opinions, and profiles. You have the perfect business to get some media attention. Personal history is relatively unknown, it's a unique business, and it's got "feel-good" appeal and automatic human interest. An article about a personal history project can encompass all the elements of a good story: drama, romance, interesting characters, and a happy ending.

It's not enough to just be a personal historian, though. The media needs an angle, so try to work your way into one. For instance, *The Wall Street Journal* was doing an article on how pre-retirees and retirees are targeting people of their own age group as customers. I fit the bill as an older entrepreneur whose typical customers are aging baby boomers and their parents, so I pitched to them and was contacted by a reporter who mentioned Heritage Memoirs and quoted me in her article.

Another time, I contacted the *Toronto Star*, Canada's newspaper with the largest circulation, which was doing a series on aging. The reporter did a feature on me and my clients, complemented by an article about how life review and reminiscence is gaining interest with health-care practitioners.

1.2 Writing a press release

To get media coverage, you have to attract a producer's or editor's attention. The normal channel for this is the press release (sometimes called a news release). Press releases are free, so there's no reason not to send one out as long as it's a good one. You might only get one shot because if an editor sees too many from you he or she won't even read them. A good press release is one that is truly newsworthy, relevant to the publication or the medium's audience, brief, and well-written. Be forewarned that editors are very busy and receive an overwhelming amount of stuff. Most of it ends up in the garbage. Make your press release stand out and capture their attention by showing them why their readers would like to know about your business, event, or story.

Some of the many ways you make yourself and your business newsworthy:

- When you're the new business in town. Write a press release about the launch of your business. This might not get you into a national newspaper, but it might very well be of interest to a local paper or magazine.

- When you can find an angle that makes the story relevant to your local community or the time of year, such as:

  - A community festival or fundraiser that you're participating in.

  - A client whose life story is relevant to a holiday such as Mother's Day, etc.

  - A mystery that was solved by doing a personal history, or a family that was reunited.

  - An upcoming workshop or speaker that you are sponsoring or in which you are participating.

1.2a Tips on writing a good press release

1. Include your contact information! Obvious, yes, but it does get overlooked sometimes. State who you are, the name of your business, its address, telephone, website, and email address.

2. Date it.

3. Make the headline in all caps, bold, and use lots of action verbs: "LOCAL WRITER WINS SCHOLARSHIP" rather than the more sedate and passive-voiced "Scholarship awarded to local writer."

4. Put all your most important information in your lead paragraph (the "lede"). It should answer the who, what, when, and where questions.

5. Remember this is for the reporter's information; it's not the place for sales talk or flattering self-promotion. Just state what your company does.

6. Send it to the right person. You can find this out with a quick phone call or by checking the masthead or website.

7. Send it to the right outlet. Read the newspaper or magazine and get familiar with the types of articles they do and who their audience is. Search their archives to see if they've just covered the topics of memoirs or family history.

8. Include a quote from yourself or perhaps a client, or someone else with whom you've worked.

1.3 Be prepared

Once you have put yourself out there, be prepared for the media to enter your world — at any time. It's not unusual for the media to contact you months after you send a press release or make an initial phone call. And they may want to interview you and send a photographer over right away. Have ready a biographical sheet, a backgrounder on personal history including some recent statistics or research, your own Q&A notes with points you might want to make (depending of course on the proposed story), and a photo of yourself.

If you have advance warning that you're going to be interviewed and have the luxury of some preparation time, try to have a dry run with a friend or your spouse or another family member. Get them to ask you tough questions and obvious questions, and practice your answers until they roll off your tongue. Just by doing this, you'll gain confidence in your abilities to talk about personal history.

If possible, ask the reporter what the story angle is beforehand, so you can prepare your answers and perhaps have some research handy. Help the reporter as much as you can by giving him or her lots of information and places to go for further resources.

1.4 Television and radio

Mega opportunity knocks when you're invited to appear on television or radio. The audience is enormous! You might get as few as 45 seconds to make your points, so again, practice and prepare as much as possible. Some things to keep in mind:

- Be aware of your body language. Shifting eyes, fiddling fingers, ramrod straight neck and shoulders — none of this conveys confidence.

- Wear something conservative and comfortable. You do not want to be distracted by a pinching earring or too-tight slacks, even for one split second.

Have a list of points you want to make. With practice, you can insert some form of these points into your answer to any question, or at least connect them to an answer with something like, "Let me give you an example," or "Along those same lines … "

For TV, it's great if you can show a real product you've completed. Having something to hold is comfortable, and eliminates the problem of what to do with your hands. Plus, it's a lot easier speaking about something tangible.

Be enthusiastic, and show it! Smile, raise your eyebrows, vary your tone, use your hands.

Relax, and remember — what have you got to lose? Enjoy your 15 minutes of fame.

2. Public Speaking: Discover Your Inner Ham

2.1 Wrestle your demons

Don't skip over this section because you have no intention of putting yourself through the agony of public speaking. I can hear what some of you are saying: It just isn't in you. You're simply too terrified and you'd make a fool of yourself. You'll find other ways to tell people about your business. I hear you loud and clear. But you can do it. If I can do it, you can certainly do it. Even the thought of speaking in front of people used to make me sick to my stomach. What helped me turn the corner was joining a theater group and finding my inner ham. After opening night of my first speaking role, during which I thought I'd be paralyzed from nerves, I found I could actually remember my lines, I could say them out loud — and act at the same time! Once you get over the first few times speaking in front of a crowd, it does get easier. Don't pass up a speaking opportunity just because it's uncomfortable at first. If you know what you're talking about, and believe it, you will be just fine.

2.2 Why it's important

Speaking to groups about life stories is a good way to get your name known, not only at the event itself but through announcements in newsletters, bulletins, websites, and newspapers. Suddenly you're becoming the expert on personal histories!

The very act of writing a 20- or 30-minute presentation will be a very useful exercise. It will help you distill all you're learning about the field into the highlights and what you deem important for people to know. This is invaluable when you're talking to potential customers one-on-one, or are called upon in an informal setting to tell people what you do.

2.3 Opportunity knocks: Suggestions for what to speak about and where to speak

You'll find many groups and organizations will welcome the opportunity to learn about personal histories, some of which might be:

- Genealogy groups
- Historical societies
- Church groups
- Service clubs such as Rotary and Optimists
- Seniors' activity centers
- Your children's school for "family history day"
- Retirement homes or adult lifestyle communities
- Retired businesspersons' groups
- Ethnic communities
- Book clubs

Giving presentations raises awareness of the field of personal history and establishes you as an expert. You may not get many clients from presentations. You may not get any; not right away, anyway. The goal is to get people to think about starting their own life stories and let them know that they can get help in many ways, such as hiring someone to organize their photos, interview them or a loved one, or edit their own already-written memoirs. Of course, some people will go home and do it themselves — either write their own memoirs or interview an elderly relative — but others may indeed call on you one day for help.

Most groups will not allow you to try to solicit business in any way. The talks are supposed to be educational and entertaining. But have lots of business cards available, and ask if you can hand them out or put them on people's chairs along with some educational information, such as a list of tips for interviewing their elderly relatives or, if the audience is elderly, some suggestions on how to start writing their memoirs. You could also ask if you can set up a display at the back of the room with your brochures and samples (watch that no one walks away with them!). Whether it's a short talk or a full workshop or course (more about these in Chapter 15), you'll want to prepare some handouts for people to take away with them. These could consist of writing exercises, a list of resources, etc., but should always have your company name and your contact information on them.

Tip: One way to make some money is to sell products at the back of the room; perhaps books that will help your audience get interested in their own personal histories. Most publishers will give you a discount if you buy a large volume. But you have to be careful you don't end up with 40 copies sitting in your basement.

Your talk should involve the audience as much as possible. Depending on the size of the group and the time you have, you could ask if anyone wants to tell a brief story about themselves; something easy and just personal enough to encourage others to share their stories, such as how they got their name. Sometimes I'll pass around a hat with some memory joggers such as "the best present I ever gave" or "the worst job I ever had" and invite people to share their memories with the group. It's not only entertaining for everyone, but it also gets them thinking about preserving their memories.

Try to get names and phone numbers of your audience to add to your contact database. With any luck, you've planted the seed of doing a personal or family history, and people might want to talk with you further. It's highly unlikely the hosting organization or institution will provide you with contact information, but what you

can do is hold a draw for a nice prize. Distribute entry cards before the presentation, and near the beginning of your talk, explain what they are and what you're giving away and invite them to enter the draw by filling out the cards you've placed on their chairs. The entry cards can have a space for their names and a place they can indicate whether or not they'd like you to contact them and give them more information on personal histories. Either way, they're entered in the draw. Ask a helper to collect the cards at the end of your presentation, perhaps during the question and answer period, and ask for a volunteer to pick a card out of a hat or bowl or whatever you've brought along. You'll be surprised at how many say that they'd like you to contact them and give you not only their name and phone number, but email address too. When you get home, be sure to call people as soon as possible and follow up on their interest.

2.3a Public speaking tips

- Remember that your audience is there because they want to be there. People are eager to listen and learn from you.

- Tell them you're a personal historian and what you do — briefly. Keep your personal journey short. People don't really care what's on your résumé and how you got to where you are.

- Start by telling them the agenda. Something like: "I have ten things I want to share with you this evening. I'll talk for about 20 minutes and then answer questions for about 10 minutes." People appreciate knowing what's in store, and when you get to point number five, they can think, "Five more to go."

- Tailor your talk to the audience. Find out as much about them as you can before your appearance. Ask the person who made the arrangements for you for any information he or she can provide. Try to find out average age, what the group would like to hear, and how many attendees will be there. Then plan accordingly.

- Find out where you're going to be speaking and what the room setup is and, if possible, go and see it. Is there a microphone? A podium? If you're using it, make sure all your technical equipment will work.

- If you must use a PowerPoint presentation, keep the number of bullet points to a maximum five per slide, and don't put complete sentences on the slides. You don't want your audience to read the slides instead of listening to you.

- Practice, practice, practice.

- If the group is elderly, you may find a few people nodding off. Don't take this personally! Ask your contact person if there's a time of day that would be best. Right after lunch is often quiet (i.e. nap time) in some assisted living or nursing homes.

- After introducing yourself, ask if everyone at the back of the room can hear you.

- Thirty minutes is a good amount of time if you're speaking nonstop. If you're involving the audience and getting them to share their stories, you could go longer.

- Have confidence, and smile!

3. Trade Shows

A trade show allows you to get your name and product in front of thousands of people in a relatively short amount of time. Trade shows — at least the big ones — are expensive, though, so do your homework. Find out how much traffic they get, what their typical visitor demographics are, if you're the only vendor of your type, etc. Also, think about if you really want to stand and greet people from 9:00 a.m. to 8:00 p.m. for several days. Do you have the budget for impressive signage, handouts, and giveaways? Do you have products to show? If the answer is "no" to any of these questions, think long and hard before you commit to the time and dollars.

If you decide it's a good thing to do, here are a few tips:

- Wear comfortable shoes and dress in layers.

- Put forward your best professional image.

- Stand beside or in front of your booth; don't sit.

- Don't read or eat at your booth. Be ready with a smile to greet your visitors and give them your full attention.

- If someone starts telling you his or her life story, shows no sign of slowing down, and is taking up all your attention, gently extract yourself and approach another visitor.

- Make sure you know what your loading times are, and where you're supposed to park and unload.

- Get there early to work out any snags before the doors open. Nothing looks worse than a vendor still setting up when the show has started.

- Ask a friend to come and fill in for you while you take a break.

- Do not leave your samples unattended. People have been known to think they're free and walk off with them!

Some things you might want to take along include:

- Business cards
- Samples
- Contact information forms
- Extension cords
- Tissues
- Bandages
- Water
- Snacks
- Scissors
- Paper towels
- Cleaning solution
- Pens
- Note pads
- Pain relievers
- Breath mints or gum

4. Local Fairs, Festivals, and Conferences

Local fairs, festivals, and conferences are often done on a much smaller scale than a trade show and more focused: for instance, a local historical society hosting a Pioneer Fair with displays of local history, photographs of family farms, or demonstrations of butter churning. A booth at an event like this could very well draw interest. You know the participants are interested in history, and you stand a fair chance of being photographed or mentioned in the local papers.

Conferences and conventions of special-interest groups allow you to connect with people who might well fall into your target market. Some conferences allow outside vendors to set

up a booth at a very reasonable cost. For instance, a genealogy conference could be a good place to tell people about your services. You know the participants are pre-qualified; they are interested in family trees, ancestry, and delving into the past. Genealogists and personal historians' professional services often overlap, and one may have occasion to hire the other. So at the very least, you might make some valuable connections and form alliances.

5. Connecting with People

Word-of-mouth is probably the number one marketing tool for personal historians, because this is a very personal business. People invite you into their homes, their families, their stories, and their lives. Customers want to hire someone they've heard about firsthand — even if the connection is by "six degrees of separation." People want to hire people they know, like, and trust. This is especially true in our business.

5.1 Face-to-face

Every marketing effort is worthwhile to try, and publicity is wonderful, but I can't stress enough how important it is that you get out there in your community and meet people face-to-face or at least talk to them on the phone. Not only are you cultivating that "know, like, and trust" vibe; you're enriching your life by meeting new people. They might bring you business or they might bring you new ideas, sources for supplies or help, information, and inspiration.

5.2 Be everywhere and be your business

Tell everyone you know what you do, and even those you don't know. Become chatty; strike up a conversation wherever and whenever you can: in the grocery store, at the dry cleaner's, with the librarian, the dentist, your kids' teachers, and the receptionist at the gym. You never know when someone will want to know more about your business. I was asked for my card while I was touring a fish research facility in Oregon, clear across the continent from where I live. One personal historian often carries around one of her sample books. When she tells someone what she does for a living and they express interest, she can whip the book out of her purse and show them. Another personal historian got a major contract when she went to a new dentist, who asked about her worklife. When she told her what she does, she said, "Interesting! Do you have a business card?" You never know when someone you meet by happenstance needs your service, or knows someone, or knows someone who knows someone, etc. But don't wait for happenstance. Get out there and make your opportunities happen.

5.3 Local connectors

Find out who the "connectors" (also known as mavens) are in your community — those people who seem to know everybody. Ask them out for coffee. If they're businesspeople they will be only too happy to make a connection with you, too. Simply say something like, "I read/heard about your business and would like to meet you to talk about ways we could possibly work together." Make your meeting friendly and brief, and be genuinely interested in their business. Ask them: "Who is your ideal customer? If I meet someone like that I'd like to be able to tell them about your business." Chances are, they will ask about your business, too. Then, keep in touch with these new contacts on a regular basis.

5.4 Referrals from former clients

Of course, the biggest source of referrals is from former clients. If clients have large families, you could see spin-off business from their siblings, children, or in-laws. If you've done a handsome book for them and they have it on their coffee table, friends and neighbors could see it and ask how they could also have a personal history done for their family. Always leave your clients with some business cards, and don't be timid. Ask if they know anyone who might need your services. When you finish a project, you might consider asking your client to fill out a brief "evaluation" that asks for the names of a couple of people you could contact.

5.5 Complementary/supplementary business colleagues

Some business might come your way from colleagues, either personal historians themselves or from complementary businesses like bookbinding, graphic design, or photography. Again, don't be shy about keeping in contact with these people and ask if they know someone who might need your services. It goes both ways: Be sure to send business their way, too.

Although not necessary, it's fairly common practice to pay a referral fee for business that comes your way from a direct referral by a colleague who could have done the work himself or herself but had to pass it on. The norm is a 5 to 10 percent referral fee. I've happily paid 10 percent for a project that I landed because another personal historian couldn't take it on; and I've in turn been paid 10 percent for sending business to other colleagues. We all spend a lot of time and money attracting leads, so we can't just give away business that results from those efforts. However, I would not expect a referral fee for passing along business to a different type of professional, such as a bookbinder. (That just goes into the category of good karma!)

5.6 Networking and working the 'Net

Networking is about building relationships, not seeing how many business cards you can hand out. It starts with making contact, getting to know a person and his or her business, and exchanging ideas, referrals, contacts, information, and resources. Think of your first contact as a pebble dropped in a pool of water, with the ripples circling outward as that person tells someone about you, and that person tells someone about you, and so on. You never know how far word will spread about your business.

5.7 Networking groups

Joining a networking group can be an excellent way to make new contacts. Businesspeople meet regularly for conversation and, hopefully, referrals. Some, like BNI (Business Network International), work on the structure of having only one professional per specialty. For instance, only one plumber, one realtor, one insurance agent, etc. Chances are, you won't find too many chapters that already have a personal historian! It's not inexpensive to join and has strict rules, but some people find BNI an effective group for getting referrals.

There are many other such groups. Some networking groups focus on the Internet, some are women-only, some are for businesses in a specific town or region. Most networking groups invite new members to come and try out the group with a free initial visit. Do your research to find a group that meets your needs and with which you're comfortable. I'd advise you to cast a wide net but then get very selec-

tive about a networking group. It might be worth joining for six months or a year but then analyzing whether it's worth your time and money to continue. If it's planting some seeds for business, or even if it energizes you or gives you a much-needed kick in the butt, great.

5.8 Relevant associations

The "must-join" organization — certainly for beginners — is the Association of Personal Historians. Some regions have regular meetings where members get together to brainstorm, explore "coopetition" opportunities (where competitors work together), swap stories, help each other resolve problems, and share resources. All this happens regularly in cyberspace, too, through an active listserv and forum. It's well worth the $200 yearly membership fee, especially if you're starting out.

Depending on your specialty or area of focus, there are likely many more associations you could join. There are groups for writers, editors, graphic designers, genealogists, photographers, scrapbookers, archivists, etc. Search around for historical societies, heritage preservationists, and oral history associations such as the International Oral History Association, the Canadian Oral History Association, and the Oral History Association. Most will have regular meetings or at least an annual conference where you can meet like-minded people.

In any networking situation, longevity is a key factor. There's a lot to be said for being in the same club or group for a number of years. It takes a long time to build relationships both in business and in every other aspect of our lives. That's why you shouldn't expect immediate rewards; be prepared to cultivate and nurture your relationships.

5.9 Make alliances

Here are just a few of the possibilities for alliances with complementary and related businesses:

- **Financial planners:** Call them up, introduce yourself, and offer to help their clients write their ethical wills (more on ethical wills in Chapter 15).

- **Scrapbooking clubs and stores:** Give a talk about telling the stories behind the photographs.

- **Law professionals:** Ask for a brief meeting, or send an information kit, to describe how you could work with them writing victim impact statements.

- **Funeral homes:** Send them information about how you could help their pre-planning clients write an ethical will or family history.

- **Genealogists:** Contact them and brainstorm about collaborating on family histories.

- **Real estate agents:** Offer your services to write the histories of houses they've sold. They foot the bill and their clients get an unforgettable, unique gift.

- **Nursing homes and retirement residences:** Give talks about preserving personal histories. Lead reminiscence group activities.

- **Eldercare professionals:** Companion services, transition specialists — Partner with them to tell the stories of their clients' heirlooms or houses they're leaving.

- **Wedding and event planners:** Offer to write the romance or tribute stories of their clients.

- **Life coaches:** Some of their clients might want to tell their life story and have it preserved.

- **Veterinarians:** Let them know you're available to do pet tribute books.

- **Photographers:** Partner with them for lavish coffee table books.

- **Hospitals, colleges, universities, religious institutions:** Write histories, tributes to founding members, famous alumni, etc.

- **Chambers of commerce/boards of trade:** Make sure they know you're available to write community histories and histories of local businesses.

5.10 Join for fun!

Whatever your interest, get out there and meet people. Join a parent council, tennis club, Rotary and other service clubs, birdwatchers, band or choir, model train enthusiasts, etc. I can hear some of you saying "No thanks, I'm not a joiner; I'm an introvert; I'm shy ... " I hear you, but if you take my advice you'll not only have a fun social time; you'll increase your potential client base a hundredfold (think of that pebble that drops in the water and the ever-widening rings). While you're at it, step forward and assume a leadership position — your profile is raised and people get to know you.

5.11 Volunteer

Know of a worthy cause? Offering your services free of charge or at a deep discount not only feels good, but it can be good for business. Your name gets known and you make valuable contacts. Here are just a few suggestions:

- Donate a two-hour oral history to a silent auction fundraiser

- Write the history of a women's shelter
- Work with hospice patients to listen and record their stories
- Preserve the stories of survivors to help heal and to preserve history
- Record the stories of family farms or heritage homes through the local historical society or museum
- Team up with a photographer to create a fundraiser book of nursing home residents showing and telling about their favorite keepsakes
- Publish a booklet of the stories of church or synagogue elders
- Sponsor an event

The possibilities really are endless!

6. Contact Management

I encourage you — I urge you — to set up a system to keep your contacts organized early in your business start-up phase. It's easy to let things slide because you think other things take priority, but after you waste a few hours trying to find the latest correspondence from a client, supplier, media contact, or colleague, you'll realize that you have to get organized and stay organized.

I'm a bit of a dinosaur and prefer a good old-fashioned filing cabinet; I just like being able to flip through real folders and pull out a piece of paper. I spend so much time on the computer as it is; I find the physical and mental process of filing papers somehow relaxing. I have folders for all clients, past and present; leads; a "good idea" file; administrative files such as tax information; good articles I've found on the Web or in the papers, etc. My email programs allow me to file important emails in folders and I must admit I get kind of lax about this. If something is really important, such as revisions from a

client, I always print it out and physically file it. However, if you prefer using your computer for your filing, you can try contact management software that integrates your contacts' information, such as email correspondence, documents, calendar, tasks, etc., syncs to your smartphone.

7. Advertising
7.1 Quantity and quality

Advertising in the wrong place is a waste of money, so do lots of probing to make sure you're reaching the right people, and a lot of the right people. Remember your market research and who your target market is. What kind of advertising do they typically respond to? Do they read seniors' newspapers that they get for free at the drugstore? Do they read glossy magazines about the latest trends? Do they belong to several online communities such as Facebook? Do they go to museums and receive the museums' newsletters? Any advertising you pay for — print, radio, TV, or Web — is expensive, so do your research before handing over your hard-earned dollars.

7.2 Making it count

Several factors influence the effectiveness of advertisements: the ad itself (creative, eye-catching), its placement in the publication or medium, and its size (or length). But what counts more than anything is the frequency with which potential customers see the ad. In printed materials, consumers typically need to see an ad at least three times to start to absorb the content and recognize it as being familiar. Many companies execute their marketing campaigns on the cost-per-thousands advertising model (CPM — the "m" is for "mille" which means thousand in Latin). CPM measures the cost of an ad for every 1,000 views, or impressions. So, if you have a low CPM in a publication with a readership that is your target market, that's a good placement, as long as you do it often enough to get noticed.

Many marketing experts agree that in general, across all media, a consumer has to hear about or read about a business sometimes dozens of times before it becomes familiar. That's why it's important that your advertising is part of a broader marketing strategy: a potential customer is much more likely to notice your ad in the paper if he or she's just heard you speak at the local arts fair, met you at a chamber of commerce meeting, or followed your car that has your business name on the back window. When I bought four consecutive weekly ads in my local paper I got two new clients, but I believe that was because an article had appeared about me the previous month. (The paper had neglected to include my contact information in the article so I thought it prudent to take out an ad.) Both new clients referred to the article.

It's wise to make consistency part of your marketing strategy. One small ad repeated every week has much greater impact than a big glossy one once a year.

12
SALES

Okay, you've got your marketing Ps all lined up: You've got the right Product and Packaging (a priceless family legacy packaged beautifully). You're in the right Place (face to face with a potential client). It's at the right Price and you are out there Promoting it. Now all you have to do is seal the deal in the all-important sales meeting.

Hold that thought. Let's back up a bit. Long before your sales meeting, there's another big "P": Preparation. Don't make the mistake of going to a sales meeting cold. By doing so, you could create a rather chilly atmosphere: not exactly conducive to closing a sale.

1. Before the Meeting: Preparation

There are several things you can do to prepare for your sales meetings.

1.1 Your sales folder

As mentioned in Chapter 9, you need a sales or presentation folder that you can leave with a potential customer or that you can send to qualified prospects. Explain the process of a personal history project. Even if you've exchanged emails and phone calls and you think your potential client understands what you do, put it in writing, in detail. Include a sales letter that introduces you and your services and how they could benefit the client and his or her family, and perhaps a sheet that outlines your pricing structure. If you've had articles published about you, or by you, include copies (obeying copyright rules for reprints), client testimonials, and some information on what a personal history is.

1.2 Your samples

Take your samples to the sales meeting. Looking at a sample book answers any questions the potential client has about format, quality, size, and all those features that are hard to imagine. It allows you to explain how you created it, step by step, and if the client has been hesitating about whether to go the whole nine yards and publish a book, this shows him or her how spoken words can be transformed into a real, beautiful book.

In rare cases, showing a sample might also work against you if the prospect can't see beyond the actual book that you're showing. It may be nothing like what he or she envisioned. It's like a real estate agent showing a house to someone and telling him or her to ignore the colors, furnishings, decor, etc.

You'll have to assess each situation yourself, but you might want to consider having the sample in your briefcase and only bringing it out if the prospect asks to see it.

1.3 Prepare yourself

Look and behave like a professional. At this initial meeting, clients will judge you based on your appearance, so dress in business clothes that are attractive but tasteful. And don't stop at your clothing. Your purse and/or briefcase should be of good quality, and clean. Take those gum wrappers and other junk out of your purse — and make sure your car is clean, too. Do whatever you need to do to be at your most confident, poised, and relaxed. Don't schedule something else until long after this meeting, so you're not watching the clock and worrying about getting there in time. Finally, remember to turn your cell phone off!

Psych yourself up. You have to want this sale. Get yourself pumped, whatever way works for you. Try doing something physical, like jumping jacks! Shout, "Yes! Yes!" Think money. What could you do with the money you'll make? Remind yourself of the value you bring to the customer; believe in what you're offering. Review some key points and write down your agenda for the meeting.

Visualize. Many top athletes, business people and public speakers and millions of others swear by the power of visualization. The concept of visualization is that when you focus on something in your mind, it seeps into your subconscious, which affects your mindset, which in turn affects your habits and behavior. Studies show that brain patterns are remarkably similar whether an action is really happening or whether it's simply being imagined. As stated in a December, 2009, article in *Psychology Today* titled "Seeing is Believing: The Power of Visualization," " … the brain is getting trained for actual performance during visualization … mental practices can enhance motivation, increase confidence … prime your brain for success." Why not try it? Close your eyes for a minute and paint a picture in your mind. Imagine the meeting going just the way you want. Run through it start to finish and picture yourself relating well to your client, impressing him or her, and closing the sale. Really try to feel the emotion that you know you'll experience as you leave the client's house with a signed contract and a check. Do this mental rehearsal often. At the very least, it will give you confidence. And you know what they say: Practice makes perfect!

Be punctual. Give yourself lots of time to get ready at home and get to the meeting place. If you're late, what does that say about your ability to manage a project? If you're early, sit in your car or take a walk until it's five minutes to your meeting time. Then it's okay to arrive at the door.

2. During the Meeting: Show Time!

2.1 Build rapport and establish parameters

As you settle in, talk about something neutral to break the ice. Resist the urge to talk for the sake of talking. Most clients don't want to hear at length about your family life, what's happening in your hometown or where you went for lunch. Keep initial chitchat about yourself to a minimum. Take your cues from your customer. Notice something about his or her house or compliment him or her on well-behaved pets. Allow the potential client to talk about something he or she knows about; realize that clients can be nervous, too. Exude an air of confidence, flexibility, and sincerity.

Begin by stating what you expect from this meeting: how long you'll spend together today, and what you see as a basic structure and end result — a mutual decision about whether what you offer is a good match for what the person needs and wants.

2.2 Establish an emotional connection

After several minutes of relaxed conversation with your client, start establishing his or her emotional connection to the project. If you can help the client see that he or she needs this family history done — and why it should be done now — most objections, even price, can be overcome. Here are a few ways to do that:

- Ask questions to gather as much information as you can. What prompted the client to contact you? Why is this project important? Is there any urgency? Has he or she tried to do it alone? Why didn't that work out (presumably it didn't; otherwise the client wouldn't be here with you)? If a client goes on about how much work has been done on his or her family history already, or that cousin Alan did a fabulous video when Uncle Al died and she's thinking Alan could also do one for her parents … listen carefully. There must be a reason he or she asked to meet you. What is it about the alternatives that isn't working? If it's not obvious, go ahead and ask, "That's great. Did it ever get finished? What challenges did you have?" Or, "How do you see me helping you, then?"

- Try to get the client to describe what he or she wants as the final product. Take notes if you want, but not at the expense of showing them how carefully you're listening.

- Assume nothing. If something's not clear, ask the client to clarify. "I'm sorry, I don't understand what you just said about _____. What do you mean?" Don't put words in clients' mouths.

- If the client gets stalled, ask more questions, and be ever more specific about the project he or she has in mind.

2.3 Talk price

There is absolutely no point in spending an hour with someone if even your lowest price is too much for them, so try to talk price early in the conversation. After the customer has talked about why he or she wants this done, ask something like, "Do you have a budget for this project?" Sometimes the client will say yes and name a number. Tuck that away for now. But sometimes you'll hear, "No. I have no idea what it would cost." At which point, if you have enough information, you can give them a range. If you don't have enough information, say "I just need to know some more details before I can give you a range for a project like this." It's important to have your prices nailed down. Even if you're charging by the hour, clients will want to know how many hours it would take — at least a range. If you name a package price range, do so with confidence. If you waver or convey nervousness through your tone of voice or body language, they will pick up on this — perhaps subconsciously — but they will notice you're uncomfortable with the way you perceive the worth of your product. At this point, if they say, "Oh. I had no idea it would be that much," you can continue by asking what they do want to spend and see what you could do for them for that amount. You have to be quick on your feet at a sales meeting and confident about what you can do for how much money. Otherwise, you run the risk of setting your price too high and closing the door completely, or agreeing to such a low amount you'll end up resentful and frustrated. I suggest you stay open to negotiation but know your limitations.

2.4 Are you talking to the decision-maker?

I have been in more than one sales meeting that lasted more than an hour, hopeful and happy that the client seemed ready to sign a contract and get started, only to have them say, "Well, I just have to run this by my sister and brothers. Jane's in Florida this week and then she's got a business trip in France ... " Or "Okay, this sounds good, but I'm not sure Mom and Dad will agree to be interviewed. I'll get back to you." More often than not, projects like this get bogged down. You want to spend your time with the one or two people who have the authority and responsibility to make decisions. So, right on the heels of your pricing talk, ask if there are any other family members involved in the decision making.

2.5 Your sales presentation

You've heard what the client wants and why he or she wants to hire you. You've learned what his or her problems are. Now it's your turn to talk and tell how you're going to design and deliver a customized solution to the problem.

Explain clearly how you work and what you could do for the client. Explain the process and watch the client for signs that he or she is not understanding. If you see such signs, ask if he or she has any questions up to this point. Do not use lingo or jargon he or she might not understand; for instance, some people might not know what it means to "transcribe an audio recording," or what's involved in scanning photographs. Give enough detail to show how much work goes into a typical project but not so much that it's overwhelming or technical.

Above all, stress the benefits and the answers to your client's problems. If a female client says that her father is ill and she doesn't want to lose his stories, assure her you can start interviewing him immediately. Tell her if you have worked with very elderly and ill people, and so you're aware of those particular challenges. If she is working full time with elderly parents, three teenagers, two dogs, and a cat, she is busy and time-stressed. Assure her that you will take care of everything. Whatever objections or roadblocks are raised, try to suggest a solution. If the cost is a big issue, explain the process and how much time goes into every project. Be sure to communicate exactly what's included in your fee and, if you've previously given a fairly wide range, narrow it down now to three price points. This gives your client a feeling of control and having a few options. Suggest which price point you feel is best for him or her and the project.

2.5a Sales dialogue

"Remember that a man's name is to him the sweetest and most important sound in any language."

— Dale Carnegie,
How to Win Friends and Influence People

There are some tried and true techniques for effective sales talk. Here are a few:

- People love to hear their names. Call your client by his or her name at the beginning of your meeting, at the end, and frequently throughout.

- Use verbal and nonverbal language to build rapport. "I know what you mean," "Me too!," and "I understand" are all powerful phrases.

- Keep it simple, positive, and enthusiastic.

- Match your body language to your words. Try a simple exercise right now. Say "I know your family will be delighted" while looking down at the floor and mumbling. Say it again, this time scratching your nose. Say it again and cast your eyes briefly to the right. Now yell it, loudly. Now go to a mirror and look yourself directly in the eye, smile, and say it again. See what I mean? Make sure your voice, body language, and words are consistent with your message.

- Be aware of the power of words. Use good words like "exclusive," "lasting," "treasure," etc. Avoid words like "contract" and "obligation." "Own" is a much nicer word than "buy," isn't it?

2.6 Closing the sale

After you're finished your sales presentation, ask if there are any questions and again, resolve any concerns. If everything seems "green

light," ask what the client would like to do next. Is he or she ready to get started? If so, great! This is an exciting moment for your client, so build on that feeling. Talk about scheduling your first interview. Talk about how excited you are to be his or her partner.

If he or she voices some objections, try to recapture the emotional involvement. You don't have to be pushy, but if, for instance, he or she says it's just not in the budget right now, remind the client that a family history costs about as much as a vacation, a lot less than a new car, and unlike something material that will deteriorate over time and have to be replaced, or that will be forgotten. A family history book will live on for future generations.

2.7 Winning a "yes" from a "no" customer

If it seems that you could lose a customer altogether — if he or she simply doesn't want to (or can't) spend as much as you quoted for the project he or she had in mind — you can try one of two things: adjust your price or adjust your product. (Well, you could also wish him or her a good day and leave, but let's assume you want this project!)

2.7a Adjust your price

Although I'm not a big fan of lowering your price, in some instances it may be worth it. You may decide you want the experience to build your portfolio and are willing to work for a lower rate. But it's tricky. You don't want to jump in too early if it's not necessary, and you definitely don't want to sound desperate. But I see no harm in offering a discount of 5 to 10 percent — if the client gives you a deposit today, or because he or she lives so close and you won't have as much travel time, or because he or she is a friend of the family, etc. This is entirely a personal decision, and some experts would balk at this, saying that if someone can spend $3,500 then they can spend $4,000, but I think that like anything else, getting a discount might just be enough to push a potential client over to a "yes" at this meeting. For this reason, you may want to consider building some wiggle room into your initial estimate or quote.

2.7b Adjust your product

Just because the client can't afford a complete life story right now doesn't mean the project is a bust. Depending on how much they want to spend, you can offer several cheaper alternatives. Here are a few suggestions:

- A one-hour interview transcribed and lightly edited, perhaps focusing on a certain aspect of his or her life.

- A number of interviews recorded and burned onto an audio CD.

- Recording him or her as he or she talks about photos. Transcribe the recordings and print them on little cards that can be glued into the photo album beside the photo (or produce a digital photo-book).

- Record your client reading his or her children's or grandchildren's favorite bedtime story.

- Scan his or her photographs and burn these on CDs.

- Create a calendar of favorite photos and include the stories behind them.

The goal, of course, is to begin a relationship with your client in the hope that he or she will hire you again at some point. Many people who are initially reluctant to do a large-scale personal history project later agree to it once they see how easy and rewarding the process is.

2.8 Contract at the ready

Always have two copies of your contract with you should the client say yes. Fill in the details about the price, and review everything. Your contract should say that a deposit is due upon signing the contract, and you should therefore receive a check before you leave. You should definitely receive a check before you start any interviews.

2.9 "No" just means "not right now"

If potential clients say "I'll have to think about it," or flat out say, "No thanks," don't take it personally. Their reasons probably have little to do with you or your qualifications. There may be internal family issues, a crisis that's taken over their priorities, they don't see the need to do it right now, they want to explore alternatives, or they're merely choosing the safer route and doing nothing. If they say no, ask if they'd like you to contact them again in six months or next year. But don't waste a lot of time and effort on people who say no. Just move on and say, "Next!"

2.10 After the meeting

After the sales meeting, whether you landed the contract or not, write a thank-you note. If it was a "no," leave the door open to future talks. Follow up with the prospect in six months or so, possibly when you've launched a product line or service that you think might interest them.

3. Sales Possibilities

Have an open mind about your services and products, and be flexible. As much as possible, tailor the product to each particular customer. Sometimes you'll end up working with a client on an entirely different project than originally planned.

3.1 Turning a $600 project into a $6,000 project

Upselling is when you persuade a client to add something on to a current purchase or opt for a more expensive product or service. (Adding items is sometimes also called "suggestive selling.") Just as you can offer to do a smaller project, you can up the ante. If the client initially contacted you to do just three hours of interviews recorded on a CD, that's great. Short oral histories are quick and relatively simple and if you do enough of them, can be quite lucrative. However, maybe the client is open to hearing about a full-scale heirloom book. Explain that with just a few more hours of interviews, you could transcribe and edit the text and turn it into a hardcover book with photographs. You've just gone from a $600 project to a $6,000 project.

Another example of upselling: You're teaching memoir-writing workshops: a basic/beginner course, and an advanced course. You charge a little more for the advanced course because you have more materials and the sessions are longer. You want to get as many of your beginners into the advanced class, so you might offer a small discount for your current students. After the advanced class, you offer a small discount on editing services for your students.

3.2 Cross-selling

A kissin' cousin to upselling, cross-selling is persuading a customer to buy a related product or service. For example, a client wants to write her own memoirs, not hire you as a personal historian to record her stories. She hires you as a coach or editor, and then you can publish her book.

Think of ways you can bundle your products and services so the "add-ons" appear to be much more valuable. Show her how it's less expensive to buy a package than if she buys each item separately; and how it's less expensive if she buys it now. For instance, if you're scanning a few photographs for a DVD, it's more efficient if you also scan a lot of photographs in the event that later on your client will want a larger project.

4. Repeat Business: Marketers Would Kill for the Information You Have

Think of the time, effort and money you spend to get one client. It is much more financially rewarding to get repeat business from a client rather than find a new client. Try to capitalize on your initial investment by getting as much business as possible from your existing client base.

As personal historians, we're in a unique position to market to former clients. We've been privy to all kinds of details about their lives — details that market research companies would pay big money for. We know ages, birthdays, anniversaries, children's birthdays, pets, religious and business affiliations, family traditions, likes and dislikes, etc. Brainstorm about how you can leverage this information (not for the market research companies!) to offer your client another product perhaps sometime in the future. Here are a few suggestions for creating repeat business from established relationships:

- You heard a woman's stories about huge family dinners where everyone would bring their own special dish. Suggest a family cookbook for everyone.

- A child's bar mitzvah is next year. How about a book about his younger years, with quotes from the elders in the family?

- Your clients' border collie is one of the family and is getting old. Maybe they'd like a collection of photographs and stories about her?

- While in a client's home, she showed you many of the family heirlooms. Why not a small book with photos of them, along with the stories behind them?

- A client's son is retiring from a distinguished career in the military. Perhaps the family would like to present the son with a tribute book?

A final word on selling. Be versatile, flexible, and resourceful. Try to anticipate what a client might ask for. For example, he or she might want to know if you can produce a video of the next family reunion. If this isn't in your product line, have some general answers ready. Find out approximately what that might cost, and get the names of people with whom you could partner. Try to avoid saying, "Sorry, I don't do that kind of thing." Wouldn't you much rather say, "Sure, I could take care of that for you," and then find out how?

5. Cold Calling

Ideally, you'll use your connections to get the names of potential clients, but that's not always possible, especially if you want to explore the possibility of working with a professional with whom you share a target market — a financial advisor, for instance, or a transition specialist who helps elderly people downsize. You just might not know anybody in that field, yet you think you could work together by providing services to his or her clients, and vice versa. Another typical scenario might be if you want to do corporate histories; you must first get a meeting with someone influential, which usually means someone in higher management.

Calling people "out of the blue" — cold calling — sends chills down some people's spines (pun intended). But if you a) have the right attitude — that is, you know you have a valuable product and service; b) accept that it's a numbers game and you'll probably get dozens of "no's" for every "yes"; and c) love a good challenge, give it a try. Again I say, what have you got to lose?

Here are a few tips for calling cold. I've used the scenario of trying to get a meeting with a businessman about doing the company's corporate history.

- Try calling offices very early (6:30 a.m. to 8:00 a.m.) or very late (6:30 p.m. to 7:30 p.m.). These are times when many executives are working but aren't bothered by other people in the office, or in a meeting.

- The first time you get voice mail or answering machine, don't leave a message.

- If you don't reach a person on the next try, leave a message but don't say what your business is. "Hi Mr. Jones. This is Mary Jane Vitality. Could you please call me back at 555-555-1515? Thank you very much. I look forward to talking with you." You probably won't get 100 percent return calls, but some people might be curious enough to wonder who you are, or even think they should remember you because you sounded like you knew them.

- A personal reference will get your foot in the door. If you don't know who in the company you should be talking to, try people high up, maybe in sales, public relations, or human resources. Introduce yourself and your business. Very likely, they'll say they are not the person you need to talk to. "I think you want to be talking to someone in Corporate Communications. Try Jack Spratt." "Okay, Jack Spratt. Thank you very much." So you call Jack Spratt's office. Maybe you get his assistant. "Hello, this is Laura Lean calling for Mr. Spratt. Christine Hammersmith in Human Resources suggested I call you." Suddenly you have a personal reference. Jack knows Christine Hammersmith, of course, and she suggested that he talk to you, which means he's probably going to take your call and find out what you're all about.

- Your goal is to discover if the person would like more information and to eventually get a meeting. If so, send your marketing packet to him with a request for an in-person meeting. Follow up in a week or so and try to set up a meeting. If, after three months, it has proved impossible to get into his office, forget the emails and phone calls and move on. In the next six months, send him a note saying you'd still like to get together. If you read an article in the paper or online that you think might be interesting, send it to him. Make sure he notices your name at least twice a year. It may seem hopeless, but think of it this way: If that company decides that it wants a corporate history written, guess who they're going to call?

- Write down what you want to say in this prospecting call. It should include your name, your business, what you do (or sell), how it benefits your customers, and an initial question to gauge interest. If there's no interest, thank the person for his or her time. If he or she opens the door, be ready with some further bits of information that show why he or she could be interested in working with you. Start with your elevator speech. "My name is Mary Jane Vitality and I'm with History in the Making. I work with companies to preserve their histories. I typically work with businesses that are celebrating milestones such as anniversaries, moving premises, or who want to pay tribute to their employees. Is this something ABC might be interested in?"

13

CLIENT RELATIONS AND CUSTOMER SERVICE: NURTURING AND MANAGING POTENTIAL AND CURRENT CLIENTS

1. Communication

From the moment you first connect with a potential client, you are in a relationship that can prosper or fail based on how well you communicate. Effective communication can help to avoid misunderstandings, resolve differences, and ensure that not only is the project successful, but also that both parties respect and like each other.

1.1 Active listening

Practice active listening in all communication: listen to (or read) what the person is saying, then say it back, summarizing your understanding of what was just said.

Client: "I'd like to meet again on the Thursday after I return."

Instead of leaving it at that, you confirm: "The Thursday after you return. Great. See you Thursday, March 11, at our usual time of 2:00 p.m."

Client: "No, no, I meant return from the cottage, not LA. I get back from the cottage on March 15."

That just saved you a wasted trip to her house on March 11!

1.2 Methods of communicating

When you start working with a new client, establish what your primary method of communication will be.

1.2a Snail mail versus email

Many seniors (and baby boomers) do not use email. You know email would be faster, but now is not the time, and you are not the person, to make this happen. Buy some postage stamps and envelopes and get reacquainted with snail mail if your client prefers it.

If your client does want to use email, though, brush up on your email etiquette. Email can be dangerous. For all its immediacy and ease, it can cause problems that can run a whole project off the rails. What you think is an efficient little note designed to not waste the time of the recipient can be misinterpreted as rude and brusque. What you think is amusing could come off as mean-spirited. Attachments forget to get attached. The email might never get to the recipient (or more likely, will go into a spam or junk folder or accidentally get deleted). Have you ever sent an email and waited and waited for a couple of weeks, wondering if you've offended the person, or he or she skipped town, or worse? You send an upbeat message — "Just wondering if you had any questions" — and discover the recipient never even received your first one.

1.2b Phone calls can have downfalls

Though baby boomers are likely to prefer email to the phone, many seniors feel more comfortable on the phone. Phone calls are personal, usually efficient at conveying information, and keep the humanity level high — if there's an issue or problem, it's best to work it out in person or on the phone. But phone calls do have downfalls. First, they can eat up a lot of time.

It's the rare phone call that doesn't include at least some chitchat, which is fine, but you have to set limits. You'll find that some clients become friends, and friends want to share news and ideas with each other. I don't want to discourage you from nurturing that relationship, but if it's taking up too much time, your other clients' projects will suffer, or, more likely, you'll end up working 12-hour days.

The second reason I don't like phone calls is simply for accuracy. If a client wants changes to a manuscript or is dictating a photo caption, I insist they send me a hard copy — not handwritten. There's just too much margin for error when you start making notes over the phone about spelling, page numbers, ages, etc.

1.3 Absences

When you start work with a client, sit down together with your calendars or business diaries and look at each other's schedules for the next month or so, and do this regularly throughout the project. Ask if they'll be away for more than a week at any time, and tell them your plans, too. This is especially crucial in the late stages of book production, when changes have to be approved and decisions made.

1.4 Frequency of communication

Establish when and how often you'll communicate. For example, will you give weekly progress reports? Will you confirm meetings a day or two beforehand? How often will you send invoices?

1.5 Honesty and openness

If you mess up and make a mistake, apologize and get it over with. You're only human. Similarly, be receptive and understanding if your client's actions result in a problem.

1.6 Conflicts

If a problem arises, do not let it simmer. You'll be working together sometimes a year or longer, on a project that's very close to the heart of your client and for which he or she is paying a lot of money. Understandably, the client will want to take ownership of it and have some control. You have to know when to loosen the reins and let the client have his or her own way. I had a client who thought he knew grammar better than I (or is that "better than me" — just kidding!), and would phone me at night to tell me that he'd "caught" another error. In a case like that, I could not let incorrect grammar go through, but if, for instance, a client wants to hold up book production for two weeks while he consults with his brother about the design — that's his prerogative. You have a lot invested in the project, too, but it's just not worth it to cause hard feelings. I find almost any problem can be resolved by talking it out. As long as you remain professional, explain possible repercussions of decisions, and remain open to the possibility that you are at fault, the project will keep on an even keel and sail through stormy seas.

1.7 Expectations

Be absolutely clear about expectations: who will do what, when, where, and how. The following are just two examples where you and your client have to understand what is expected of the other:

- When you meet for interviews, agree on the agenda for the meeting. Schedule the date and time of the next meeting and if it needs to be changed, agree that you will let the other person know at least two days in advance.

- When you send the first draft of the manuscript, ask if the client will be able to return any changes to you within x number of weeks; if not, when? If the client doesn't return it to you by then, you can't guarantee a delivery date of x. You might have reserved a graphic designer who's waiting for the manuscript, whom you'll now lose because the manuscript won't be ready for another two months and the designer can't fit you into his or her schedule. The client has to understand the ramifications of changes. You don't want to overwhelm a client with details and too much information, but keep the lines of communication very open and remind him or her often of deadlines and what you agreed to, and what they can expect to happen if there are too many extensive unplanned changes.

2. The Many Hats of Customer Service

As a personal historian in your own business, you'll wear many hats. As you switch from one to another, keep in mind that every role and every task should be geared toward satisfying your clients.

Just for fun, I've suggested how, when you're wearing one of your many hats, you can deliver stellar customer service.

Executive Assistant Hat: Return phone calls and emails promptly; maintain efficient filing system; avoid scheduling conflicts.

Salesperson Hat: Understand and respond to customers' needs; tailor a product and service accordingly. Deliver what is promised. Price the products fairly.

Editor's Hat: Respect clients' words; make changes cheerfully; ensure accuracy and uphold excellent editorial standards.

Designer's Hat: Listen to clients' preferences; incorporate clients' personalities into design.

Production Manager's Hat: Use top-quality material and methods to deliver superior product.

Marketing Director's Hat: Identify target market; be proactive in marketing efforts. Anticipate what will satisfy the customer, what will make him or her happy, what will make him or her a repeat customer or refer you to friends. Plan campaigns that attract new customers and build loyalty among current and past customers. Maintain website and other tools to create a satisfying, educational start to the personal history process.

Bookkeeper's/Accountant's Hat: Prepare invoices in a professional format. Promptly deliver receipts of payment. Keep accurate records of time, expenses.

Operations Manager's Hat: Act as project manager when needed; see big picture and goals. Ensure an efficient workflow by anticipating and managing staff requirements. Maintain good relationships with partnering companies. Keep office environment clear of clutter to maximize efficiency.

Public Relations Hat: Send cards and thank-yous to customers. Keep in frequent contact to let customers know they are your #1 priority. Remember details about clients that make them feel special.

3. How Can I Wow?

You've probably heard this saying: Underpromise and overdeliver. Be very realistic about saying what you can do; hold back a bit so that your client's expectations are surpassed, not merely met. Refrain from an enthusiastic but perhaps overly optimistic claim such as, "I'll bet we can get this book ready in time for your parents' anniversary!" When a promise or claim is not delivered, it makes customers unhappy and disappointed, and that's not good for anyone. However, imagine if the customer wasn't expecting the book until two weeks after the anniversary party, and you surprise them by delivering a day before the party so all their parents' friends and family can sign a copy. Happy customer! Always build in a cushion of comfort to allow for the "overdeliver" factor, as well as to allow for inevitable hiccups and delays.

3.1 Let's give them something to talk about

What makes you enthusiastically recommend a product, restaurant, or store to your friends? It's usually something special, something out of the ordinary. Try to think of ways you can go the extra mile for your clients.

Here are a couple of examples that demonstrate the power of both great and lousy customer service. In the 1970s, one of my clients sponsored a Vietnamese refugee family and took them shopping. The staff were excited to see this family of "boat people" in their store. As my client and the family were leaving, one young saleswoman ran to the back room, came up to them and gave one of the new immigrants her own sweater, because "winter is coming and you'll need it." My client has mentioned the kindness of that sales clerk and the store — which is still there —to all her friends for almost 40 years.

At the other end of the spectrum: A man was having lunch at a major chain restaurant where he was served a soft drink that had a piece of broken glass in the bottom of the glass, which he sucked up through a straw and which cut his lip pretty badly. He got his drink replaced and they brought him a Band-Aid; that's it. No manager apologized, no free meal, not even a free drink. This man is a workshop leader for a large communications firm, and figures he's told at least 900 students that story, and of course he names the restaurant. Those 900 will probably tell another 900, and so on. Bad for business. Now, if that restaurant had given him not only a free drink but a free meal and a coupon for at least one more, he might not be badmouthing them to hundreds of people years after the fact.

Ask yourself, how can my customer service be so amazing that my clients won't be able to stop talking about me — in a good, "WOW!" way?

14
TIME MANAGEMENT AND PROJECT MANAGEMENT

1. Time Management

Whether you're running a part-time or full-time business, you have to make the most of your working hours. If you don't, you risk making a part-time income while putting in full-time hours!

All the software and computer programs in the world can't help you manage your time wisely if you don't have the right attitude and self-discipline.

1.1 Stay focused on the real priorities

There is much more to running a business than working on a particular project. Among the dozens of responsibilities are: cleaning and organizing your office, paying bills, invoicing, computer maintenance, marketing, buying supplies ... all those necessary tasks that aren't likely to get the adrenaline pumping, like starting work with a new client does.

Remember all those customer service hats I mentioned in Chapter 13? Every one of them takes time. It's tempting to let those tasks slide, because a) you're not answering to anyone but yourself; b) some of them aren't making you money (directly); c) they're not as interesting or creative as some of your other work; and d) some of them — like reminding a client that payment is due or spending an hour on the phone with service people over an Internet problem — are unpleasant or irritating. But they must be done, so don't put them off.

1.2 Recognize your work habits

Are you the type of person who expands the work to fit the time allowed to do it? Say, for example, you have to get a file to the printer by Wednesday at noon and it's now Tuesday morning. You figure it's going to take you three hours to prepare the file and send it. But you end up working on it for five rather unproductive hours on Tuesday and two more semi-productive hours on Wednesday morning. How could you have made better use of your time?

One way would be to give yourself a false deadline of having the file ready by Tuesday at 3:00 p.m. Another would be to do something else on Tuesday, and work hard and uninterrupted on the file on Wednesday morning. If you work best when faced with a deadline, recognize that and schedule your time accordingly. Don't expand the work to fill a space, just because you have it.

1.3 Take a break

Sometimes you have to work smarter, not harder. My best work is done when I'm energized, and I feel like I'm attacking the work, not slogging through the muddle of my tired brain. Take several breaks to get out of the moment and do something totally unrelated to work: walk the dog, call a friend, go to the gym, paint a chair, and so on. You'll return to your desk with a fresh perspective and probably some new ideas.

1.4 Email and the Internet: The great time wasters

You cannot afford to waste time doing things that don't advance your business. If you got up from your desk and went to watch a soap opera for an hour, you'd know that you were not working, right? But think of how much time you spend flipping through websites that have very little to do with your business. You may tell yourself that you're learning something new that will come in handy with a client one day, or that writing a long email to a former colleague is valuable networking. Try to keep these things to a reasonable limit. If you're curious as to how much time you're wasting, try keeping a diary for a few days and mark down any time you spend on email and surfing the Web that is not directly helping your business.

Set aside three times a day when you'll check email. Then close and quit your email program. Otherwise you might get, like I do, a tempting little envelope when there's new mail. Try as I might, as focused as I can be on writing something, that little envelope beckons and I give in. Click. Oh, it's so-and-so! She sent pictures of the reunion last week. Click. Click. Save. Create New Folder. Look at a couple of other photos in iPhoto. Think about a new photo for my LinkedIn page. Close iPhoto. But must respond and thank so-and-so … there it goes, 15 minutes gone. But it's not just 15 minutes; experts say it can take anywhere from 25 to 60 minutes to recover your concentration.

When you do check your email, leave the personal messages until a dedicated time. If an email looks like it's from a potential client or is from a current client, I do open it, and if I can deal with the query in two minutes, I do that. If it's going to require any more than two minutes, I mark it "Unread" and get back to the task at hand.

Tip: Get an email account through Gmail, Hotmail, or another web-based company for your personal messages. Keep your business email separate and don't junk it up with all those forwards from well-meaning friends and special offers from your cell phone company.

2. Project Management

2.1 Schedule your projects

Plan ahead as much as possible. Look at the various tasks involved in each project and allot enough time for each. Because of the variety of tasks involved in putting together a personal history, it's entirely possible to be working on several projects at any given time. For example, you can do an interview in the morning and do editing in the afternoon. You can speak at a Rotary Club meeting in the morning and do an interview in the afternoon. But what you can't do is two interviews in the same morning when your clients live an hour away from each other.

Tip: Any schedule is flexible. Go easy on yourself if a deadline is stressing you out. If you have to reschedule, do so, and give yourself time to do the job properly.

2.1a Taking on new projects

When you're asked to start a new job, be realistic about your time. Your client will probably want to start immediately, but you may already have more work than you can handle for the next six weeks. Don't panic and think you're going to lose the contract if you say you can't start for another month or so. The fact that you're so busy might actually impress him or her!

2.2 Plan your projects

For each new project, do a simple project management plan. Write down the tasks you know you'll need to do, approximately how long they will take you, and when you think you'll complete them. As you work on the project, write down the actual dates and how long it really took you. This not only keeps you on track; it helps you plan for future projects.

2.3 Track your time

Whether you're working on a package price or you're charging by the hour, it's very important to keep track of your time. For each project, keep an Excel sheet where you enter the date of the task, what it was, and how long you spent on it. For your own record keeping and business planning, mark whether it was for planning, administrative tasks, interview preparation, interviewing, research, travel, transcribing, editorial, scanning, design, correspondence/consultation with client, or subcontracting. Not only does this give you an accurate total of how much time you actually spent on that particular project, but it will help you in your planning and estimating for future projects.

2.3a Billable versus non-billable hours of a project

From the time you are first contacted by a client to the cashing of your final check, you could work hundreds of hours on a project. If you're billing by the hour, what exactly can you bill for?

These are the tasks I consider non-billable:

- Initial contact, whether by email, phone, or in person, where I explain my services and learn a bit about the project

- Learning new software or installing programs; clients shouldn't have to pay for my learning curve or maintenance

- Background research that I do for my own education into the client's life and times. Just because I don't know about a certain period in history doesn't mean the client should pay me to learn about it.

- My own slip-ups

- Preparing a proposal or quote

Billable hours include everything else, including consultation with family members; consultation with designers, printers, and binders; labelling CDs; reviewing documents returned from a transcriber, etc.

2.4 In sickness and in health

If you've ever been employed on salary at a company, you probably got paid on those days when you weren't feeling well. Maybe you weren't as productive as usual or had to phone in sick. Working on your own, you'll have days when you aren't feeling well, too, but there's no boss to phone. You'll probably try to push yourself to get things done no matter how you're feeling. Sometimes this will work, even though you're only 50 percent productive, but other times you'll just have to turn the computer off and take to the couch, hopefully with a kind "assistant" to bring you tea and chicken soup. Be good to yourself and take the time you need to recuperate. You're not doing your best work, so rest up until you're back on your feet. This is when you'll be glad you have a support system in place, whether it's a family member helping around the house and making that chicken soup, a friend to vent your frustration to, or a colleague who can step in with some paid assistance.

2.5 Work flow

Having multiple projects can be both stimulating and stressful. Tip the scales toward the former by managing your work flow intelligently.

2.5a Stay organized

I can't emphasize enough how important it is to stay organized. Here are just a few traps to avoid:

- Printing emails, articles, and documents, then putting them aside for filing "later."

- Mixing personal paperwork like home electricity bills with business documents.

- Relying on memory instead of writing it down or entering it in your business diary or computer.

- Confusing important tasks (those that have to be done) with urgent tasks (those that have to be done immediately). Prioritize, and stay focused.

Take the time to set up your systems and keep them organized, and your work will go a lot smoother. Your electronic files should be organized in a way that you can easily find things. Sounds obvious, doesn't it? But consider this scenario: You find a useful article on the Web that you want to save, and you're in a hurry, so you plunk it into your Marketing folder. All is well and good, except your Marketing folder also holds folders called Publicity, Promotion, an odd assortment of files like the registration form for a trade show that you never attended, and a list of advertising rates for the local paper. Two months later, when you want to reference that useful article, you'll spend 15 minutes looking for it.

Trash those outdated files. You'll probably have several versions of documents and several duplicates. Be careful not to throw the baby out with the bathwater, though. Even after a project is over, save your most important files for a good amount of time. You never know when a client might want to update a project, so you'll need those electronic files.

2.5b Keep a business diary

Keep a diary of your business activities. Write down what you did all day — it's a great feeling when you look back over past weeks and see how busy you were and what progress you made! Look to the days and weeks ahead and write yourself reminders of what you have to do; everything from sending birthday cards to following up with a prospective client. Before you quit work for the day, turn to the next day's date and jot down what you want to accomplish. When you have what seems like an overwhelming number of things to do, writing them down somehow makes them a lot more manageable.

2.5c Think ahead

Try to anticipate what you need before you come to a particular task, so that you're ready. For instance, you remember that the last time you were editing, you had some trouble formatting en dashes and em dashes. Find out how to handle those before you start editing, and write down the instructions.

Also get your team in place, early. For instance, if you know you're going to need a transcriber in the next few months, ask about his or her availability well in advance.

For each project, keep a style sheet or guide. Write down correct spellings of places, names, etc., and make a note of what style you're using.

2.5d Keep it moving

If you're referring to your project plan and keeping a list of to-dos in your business diary, you should be able to anticipate possible snags and deal with them before they happen. Here are a few pitfalls to watch for:

- If you haven't received something you're waiting for, whether it be a signed contract, photos, or revisions, follow up within a reasonable timeframe. As I mentioned earlier, communication is crucial. Tell your client or subcontractor when you'd like the material back and if that is not possible, ask them when they can return it to you. Then follow up at that time.

- Don't let audio recordings build up. If your transcriber is too busy, find another one. Ideally, you've reserved your transcriber's time and given him or her a heads-up to expect your file by an approximate date. If one has let you down, think about finding someone else. This goes for all subcontractors. You can't afford to risk the success of a project on an unreliable subcontractor, even if you've had a long relationship. Demand as much of other people as you do of yourself.

- Similarly, don't let any task build up to the point where it's overwhelming. Make a list of priorities and feel the satisfaction as you cross things off the list. That alone will energize and motivate you. If you need a break, take it.

Maximize the time you spend on setup and preparation so that you're not needlessly repeating tasks. For instance, schedule a good chunk of time for certain tasks such as scanning photos. It is much more efficient to spend an afternoon getting them all done than to set up the scanner and open all your folders and files and only get 20 percent done and have to repeat it five times.

I don't start the major edit of a manuscript until all the transcripts are complete, but once I start, I like to put aside any distractions and focus on that one project. But scheduling is sometimes hard to do because of the many variables in this business: people getting ill, snowbirds going south for the winter, photographs or documents that have to be retrieved from a cousin in Australia ... but try to anticipate and set aside the time you need for big, time-consuming tasks. I have my "juggling days" when I do ten different things from running to the post office to answering queries, to my "put on the blinders" days when I don't even answer the phone or check email.

2.6 Managing difficult clients

2.6a Handle criticism with professional grace

The cliché is true: You can't please all of the people all of the time. No matter how hard you try, there will be clients who find fault. That's business. Personal historians tend to be sensitive and caring. When a client complains about something, or withdraws from your relationship, sometimes it's hard not to take it personally. As a businessperson, though, you have to develop a thick skin and realize that you are still a hired hand, even though you think you're doing saintly work! Sometimes, no matter how clearly you've communicated what your services are, what the final product will be, how you work, etc., there will be misunderstandings. Clients can make unreasonable demands, such as revising something four or five times. You need to set your own limits and decide how long you'll grit your teeth and just do it, and when you've had enough and tell the client his or her requests have exceeded the boundaries of your agreement and you have to start charging for your time. You might just find the client is more than happy to pay you. In fact, he or she just assumed that's how it would work. Again, communication is the key.

2.6b Set boundaries

Difficulties can arise in many other forms, too. Your client may take the relationship too personally. He or she might call you at home at inappropriate times, or even behave inappropriately. He or she may be lonely or grieving the loss of a spouse, and you may spend too much time in your sessions consoling or listening to this person talk about things he or she has no intention of putting in the memoir. Deal with these situations as the professional you are. Seek advice if you need it. If you're uncomfortable, trust your instincts and gently extract yourself from the project.

2.6c Breaking up is hard to do

There may be occasions when you have to walk away from a project — either one that has yet to start, or one that's underway. If working with a client is taking a serious toll on you, personally or professionally, it's time to end it. Here are a few possible scenarios:

- You've spent four hours talking or emailing with a potential client, and another hour preparing a proposal and quote. The client seems to still want to hire you, but one roadblock after another appears and months, or even years, go by and you still don't have a contract. Whatever the reasons, it seems as if the client just wants to talk about it for another year or so without the commitment.

- Your client is revealing things about himself or herself that you cannot tolerate (morally or otherwise).

- Your client finds fault with just about everything you do.

Any of the above reasons could be enough for you to want to say goodbye to a client; if you need to do so, don't be wishy-washy in your language. Make it very clear that you cannot continue with the project. Stay professional. Don't let your emotions run away with you in any discussions, either in person, on the phone, or in an email. Keep an even tone, explain your reasons, and thank the client for the opportunity to work with him or her. Ending a relationship is never pleasant, and when you have a legal agreement with a client, it can be messy. Be sure to protect yourself in your contract by including a clause that says the contract can be terminated by you with two weeks' notice, or whatever you determine as fair or necessary.

15
GROWING
YOUR BUSINESS

1. Expand Your Offerings

The beauty of a personal history business is that you can adapt your expertise to a number of areas. Try different products and services and see what your bestsellers are, and which ones you like to do. In this chapter I describe a few of the many exciting possibilities.

1.1 Questions of the heart and soul: Ethical wills and legacy letters

Ethical wills, or legacy letters, are a natural extension of your personal history business offerings. I call this section "questions of the heart and soul" because ethical wills express a person's deepest, most heartfelt thoughts and feelings about what's important to them — what matters. Ethical wills are an ancient Judeo-Christian tradition, noted in both the Hebrew and Christian bibles as a way of passing beliefs, values, blessings, and moral direction from one generation to the next. Today they are also known as legacy letters and are used by people of all faiths (or no faith, as the case may be). Unlike a last will and testament, or a living will that dictates wishes about medical issues, an ethical will is not a legal document. It's a letter or a statement expressing what you want your loved ones to know about you: your beliefs, values, guiding principles, life lessons, wishes, hopes and dreams for your family and descendants, how much you loved them, what was important to you, or how you want to be remembered. It can be as long as a book or as short as a paragraph and can take many forms: a letter, a poem, a song, a multimedia presentation ... it is the ultimate in personal expression, so the author can be as creative as he or she wishes. A legacy letter can be written at any stage of life by anyone who wants to ensure that their values live on, and can be updated at any time. It can be read and shared among family members, or sealed until the writer dies.

Just a few ways legacy letters are used can include the following:

- Parents write a letter to their children every year on their birthdays, saying what the last year has meant to them and how their child has developed and grown.

- Founders of family firms document the ethics the company was built on and which they hope their heirs will uphold as they take over the firm.

- A parent who is dying writes love letters to each of his or her children, parents, and spouse.

- Elderly adults express their love to their children and grandchildren.

- Parents explain the decisions they made in their legal will: who received what, and why, or their wishes for how the money will be spent.

As a personal historian, you could develop an income stream helping people compose their legacy letters. (Many personal historians incorporate this type of material within a larger personal history book. Sometimes clients also wish to have another, more extensive version of their legacy letter published in a separate format.) Some questions you might ask include:

- What principles have guided you through your life — or what have you tried to uphold?

- If you could bequeath $500,000 among five different charities, which would you choose and why?

- What is your favorite place in all the world and why?

- What's the most important thing your parents taught you?

- What brings you the most joy?

- What do you wish for your children and descendants?

- If you were to die today, what would be your biggest regret?

- What do you want your family to know about you?

- What do you want your family to know about your religious faith? Your beliefs and values?

See Sample 17 for examples of ethical wills.

Dr. Barry Baines is a pioneer in this field and a colleague in the Association of Personal Historians. His website, www.ethicalwill.com, has extensive resources, and he holds workshops in facilitating ethical will documentation. Dr. Baines granted permission to print an excerpt from an ethical will written by his father one month before he died (see Sample 17).

And on another, lighter note, here's an excerpt from a fifteenth century ethical will called "Instructions to a Son."

In 1660, while imprisoned in the Tower of London awaiting beheading for high treason, the Marquess of Argyll wrote "Instructions to a Son" for his son, Archibald, who would become the next Chief of Clan Campbell. Here is his advice about marrying a woman much older or younger than yourself:

"As you match your peer in honour, let her be so in years; a difference in age is a secret fire raked up for a time which will afterwards break out and consume your quiet;

ETHICAL WILLS

1. Barry Baines' father

The following ethical will was written by Barry Baines' father when he was 70. He died of lung cancer about one month after this was written.

Dear Barry and Sandy:

A few words to express my feelings and thoughts while time is running out on me.

Some standard values that I have basically lived by throughout my life, are that I have always believed in honesty and advocated truthfulness. I cherish the family with all my heart. I always felt that I gave of myself to everyone in the family. The satisfaction and gratification that I received in return is in the accomplishments of my children. No father could be as proud as your father is of you. Throughout your lifetime so far, you have more than exceeded my greatest expectations. You continue to move forward in a manner that makes me love you more and more. I'm proud to say, "That's my son!"

Through the years, I've tried to take care of my family and give them some of the better things in life. I tried and succeeded in being able to give my children a good education. Although I was only a working man, many was the time I worked two jobs for the extra money so that the family could have a little bit more. I had often thought of going into some kind of business, but I didn't have the expertise in any particular field, or the finances to afford the luxury of risk. However, I'm proud to say that you have shown me through the years, the aggressiveness that I lacked emerged in you.

I have tried to be financially sound and leave behind an adequate amount of finances to carry your mother through the rest of her days. Being that no one can predict the future, I ask that should it ever be necessary, see that your mother remains comfortable financially and otherwise.

Sandy, you have always made me proud with your accomplishments and different endeavors. You have never undertaken a task that was underachieved. Through the years you have been in my confidence and as close as a daughter. I love you and the girls deeply.

My concentration is not too great at this point as I'm sure I can say much more. Barry could not have picked a finer mate. You are a good wife and excellent mother. I feel a father and daughter relation to you.

I hope Alisha and Hannah follow in the footsteps of the family and their traditions. I love you all.

Dad

2. Bettina Brickell

Bettina Brickell was 29 years old when she died. This letter to her family and friends was read at her memorial service.

Dear Friends and Loved Ones,

As I contemplated this memorial service, I felt great gratitude in my heart that each of you would be here to say goodbye to me. Many of you have shared your warmth, kindness, and love with me during these last months. I want to say thank you and goodbye and share with you the lessons I've learned through my dying.

I have profoundly experienced that love is all that matters. Like many people, I occasionally got caught in my pettiness and separation, thinking I knew the right answer. I judged others and I have judged myself even more harshly. But I have learned that we carry within ourselves the abundant wisdom and love to heal our weary heart and judgmental mind.

During the time of my illness, I have loved more deeply. My heart feels as if it has exploded. I do not carry anger. I feel we are all doing the best we can. Judging others closes the heart and when one is dying, that is a waste of precious sharing. Life is how we stand in relationship to both ourselves and to others. Loving and helping each other are all that is important.

We are in the fall season. I feel privileged to die as the leaves fall from the trees. There is a naturalness to the cycle of life and death and for whatever reason, it is my time to die, even though I am young. It is okay. It is right and natural. Life is not about how long we live, but about how we live, and I have had a good life. I accept my dying as part of the wondrous process of life.

My sadness is in leaving you. I'll miss the deep comfort and love of gently waking up in my husband Peter's arms, giving up our dreams of future years together. I'll miss the sunny days of fishing with my dad, of sharing with my mom her love of life and cosmopolitan savoir-faire. I'll miss giggling with my sister, Maria, over life's impasses. How appreciative I feel when I think of my brother Michael's faith in and encouragement of me …

As I lay dying, I think of all of you, each special in your own way, that I have loved and shared this life with. I reluctantly give up walking on this beautiful planet, where every step is a prayer. The glistening sun on the trees, the sound of a brook as it makes its way down the mountain, the serenity and beauty of a gentle snowfall, sitting at the rim of a Utah canyon and catching a glimpse of eternity — these are the things I have loved.

Please do not think I have lost a battle with cancer, for I have won the challenge of life. I have shared unconditional love. I have opened to the mystery of Spirit and feel that divinity is all around us every day and provides us with a path on which our spirit may take flight.

Chief Crazy Horse said upon his final battle, "It is a good day to die because all the things of my life are present." That is how I feel as I think of the abundance, adventure, opportunity and love in my life.

When you think of me, know that my spirit has taken flight and that I loved you.

With my love, Bettina

when either of your desires and strength answer not the vigour of the youngest, then the sparkles will fly by such violent collisions and clashings that will soon set your family in combustion."

Let's hope Archibald took his father's advice and avoided the violent collisions, clashings, and combustion!

An ethical will or legacy letter is not a legal last will and testament. It's what the author wants his or her family to know, not have.

1.2 If these walls could talk! House or heritage building histories

1.2a Heritage buildings

There was a time when, in the name of progress, old buildings were demolished in favor of box-like structures with no character or architectural interest. Now, thankfully, there are measures to protect some of these fine buildings, but some are still in danger. Documenting and saving the history behind them could provide fundraisers with meaningful stories in a tangible format. Not only might you contribute to the preservation of the building but its history is now documented forever.

1.2b B&Bs, hotels and inns, resorts

If those walls could talk, what stories we'd hear. Some bed and breakfasts, hotels, inns, and resorts are steeped in history and have fascinating stories attached to them, and tourists seek them out for that very reason. Help the owners of these establishments leverage their appeal by researching the buildings' or the businesses' stories. Put them together with photos, both old and new, in a handsome brochure or book. Include some recipes from the kitchen for a homey, practical touch!

1.2c Houses

Homeowners who buy old houses probably aren't interested in finished basements and en-suite bathrooms. They want to "own" the story behind the house — who lived there, who built it, its architectural style, changes over the years, and its history. A book with photos and stories would be a wonderful gift for new homeowners!

You can find out who lived in a house by researching city directories (as they are called in North America; they're called street directories in Britain, New Zealand, and Australia. In Canada they are referred to by either name). City Directories often list the occupation of the resident as well as where they worked. What history! You can also search archives, Land Titles offices for the names of the owners (who were not always the tenants), and fire insurance maps such as those created by the Sanborn Company. Certainly people whose houses are on a Historic Tour might well be interested in creating some form of brochure, booklet, or book.

1.3 Corporate or business histories

More and more businesses are realizing the importance of documenting their history and celebrating their heritage and unique corporate cultures. Business histories help a company leverage its brand with customers and suppliers, unite and rally employees, celebrate milestones, and ensure their history is passed down through the generations. In tough economic times, it's a way to show customers they have weathered challenges before, and they're "built to last." Using your interviewing, writing, and editing skills, you can tell the stories of the company and the people.

If you're cold calling, first try the departments of public relations, human resources, corporate communication, or marketing. Or, go straight to the top and try to get a meeting with the president or CEO. Put together a professional package with some information about yourself, reasons why the company should do a business history, and some excerpts from reviews about other business histories. If their competition has done one, that might be worth mentioning!

Corporate histories are much larger projects than an individual's life story, of course. You'll be researching a company's archives (which you can only hope have been organized and stored properly); looking through old newspapers and magazines for articles about the company; sifting through photographs and trying to identify people and places; interviewing perhaps dozens or hundreds of people; working with staff members; and otherwise managing a huge project.

Tip: For help in researching a local or business history, a win-win option is to hire a high school or college student. The student gains experience and earns some money, and you get assistance at a discount.

When doing a company history, be sure to keep your contact at the firm regularly updated to make sure you're on track and covering everything the firm wants included, that you're within budget, and the timelines are being met — and if they're not being met because they're held up at their end, make sure they're aware of that. Talk to the key people at the firm about their priorities for this project — what their objective is, important things you should know, and the people you should interview. Interview current and former employees, suppliers, customers, and get a good cross-section of people, from the president to the warehouse packers. If it's a large company or a company with a presence in the community, you could probably get local media involved in asking the public to loan their memorabilia or agree to be interviewed.

By their very nature and scope, corporate histories can pay very handsomely.

1.4 Family reunions

Generations getting together to celebrate family — what a great opportunity to gather stories! Go armed with your recorder, camera, and notebook and interview as many people as you can corner. Since some reunions attract hundreds, you could potentially sell a lot of books (or DVDs). One way to find upcoming reunions is to ask at resorts and hotels that advertise themselves as popular venues. Try teaming up with event planners.

1.5 Community/local histories

With the surge of interest in genealogy, and the Internet making research easier, local histories are popping up everywhere. There's a new aura of nostalgia about the way things were, and you can capitalize on it. Doing a local history will raise your profile in the community and put you in contact with hundreds of people, and could easily lead to spinoff personal and family histories. That's a good thing, because the local histories themselves can be big projects that may or may not pay you adequately. Try to get financial assistance through a grant from local, state, provincial, or federal sources, or sponsorship from businesses or associations.

For sample local history interview topics, see Sample 18.

When taking the helm of a local history project, you can follow basically the same process as that of a first-person memoir, but amplify it about 1,000 times. You will be working with either paid staff or volunteers, community leaders, officials, as well as the many people whose stories you want to gather. These are big projects that require careful planning, excellent and supportive teamwork, and a timeline that may be as long as three years. You'll need to do a lot of research, through museums, archives, business records, newspapers, government documents such as tax rolls, census records, immigration records and vital statistics, historical societies, church and parish records, postal records, land records, firsthand accounts, private written documents, and other sources.

Local histories can include the histories of cities, towns, rural areas, regions, streets, neighborhoods, events, clubs, churches, First Nations or Native American reserves, and businesses — any community that wants to honor, celebrate, and preserve their heritage.

1.6 Engagement and wedding books

Tell the stories of the bride and groom, from their childhoods right on up to their engagement or wedding. Gather stories from their families and friends. And, of course, lots of pictures of the happy couple! Again, this is an area where partnering with an event planner makes good sense.

1.7 Memorial books or books of remembrance

Invite friends and loved ones to tell their favorite memories about someone who's passed away. Many funeral homes offer this service but their books are usually exceedingly expensive, so if you can present an affordable alternative you might find a niche. Marketing to this segment is tricky, though. You may not be comfortable calling up a family who've just lost a loved one.

1.8 Pet tributes

Every pet owner loves to tell stories about four-legged furry friends. Partner with a photographer to get some great portraits, and together with these and other photos, create a book with the family's stories about the pet.

1.9 Videobiographies

A videobiography brings a new dimension to the life story. A team of producers, directors, camera operators, makeup artists and hairstylists, editors, researchers, and lighting and sound technicians work together to interview the narrator, edit the footage, and integrate it with music, photographs, special effects, and even old home movies.

2. Teaching Life-Writing Workshops

Consider giving longer, more in-depth courses or workshops that teach people who want to write their own memoirs. (Chapter 11 covers giving presentations to various groups about the importance of preserving your life story. This section is about teaching.)

2.1 Length and venue

Memoir-writing workshops can be as short as a half-day or as long as a week-long retreat, or somewhere in between. They can even be held online through email or a webinar (a seminar on the Web). You can present them in a venue of your choice, or through an institution such as your school board's continuing education department. If you're teaching a course through a school, college, or university, it will likely have to fit into their semester system, perhaps held one evening per week for eight weeks.

Do your research before you commit to teaching a workshop or course. Make sure it will pay you adequately for your time, and choose the right audience. Though an older seniors' residence might seem like the perfect place, you might find there is little or no interest from the residents, or that there are too many challenges

INTERVIEW OUTLINE FOR SAMPLE COMMUNITY/LOCAL HISTORY

Early Days in Bakerville Local History Project:

The scope of the project has been determined: e.g., "Early Days" has been defined so the time period is known; a list of interviewees has been developed; a timeline for completion of phases, etc. These are some of the topics the interviewers could cover.

Interview Outline

- Physical location
- Where did the name Bakerville come from?
- Earliest settlers
- Early businesses
- General memories of downtown: residences, inns, hotels, pubs, restaurants, schools, churches, parks
- Social activities
- Founding fathers and mothers
- Scandals and disputes
- Demographics: e.g., racial mix, ethnic make-up, economic
- Changes over the years
- Effects of plant closing, the Depression, new business, tourist center (beach area development)
- Town traditions

with that age group, such as not being able to use a computer for their writing. Challenges can be overcome, of course, but if you need to get homework assignments emailed to you, or you plan to publish an anthology of the group's writing, you'll run into time-consuming problems.

2.2 Pricing

Teaching workshops is a great way to become known as an expert in the field. They can also be lucrative if you find a place to hold them that's reasonably priced, and if you attract enough people. The good news is that your costs can be low — just enough to cover the cost of your handouts, if you have any. Depending on your arrangement and size and budget of the venue, you could either charge a per-person fee per class or per session, or be paid directly by the school or institution. The advantage of going through a community college or university or library is that they will likely do a lot of the marketing themselves — e.g., listing the class in their calendars, collecting fees, etc. Once the class is over and you've started people on writing their memoirs, you may find that some people want to hire you for editing or coaching help, or help them publish their work.

2.3 Preparation

I guess it's possible, but it seems improbable that you could be an effective memoir teacher without having written or at least started to write your own. To this end, you should take a memoir-writing class, to not only work on your own story but to see how other workshop leaders do it. To add to your confidence level, you might consider taking a course in teaching adults. That said, however, you might find yourself being more of a leader than a teacher, as workshops are best when they include a lot of participation.

There are hundreds of books, magazines, and websites about memoir writing (see Resources section on the CD-ROM) and there are thousands of published memoirs. Read both the good and the bad and analyze what makes a memoir truly meaningful and memorable — and readable.

2.4 Environment

Workshops are usually hands-on, where you give the group writing exercises to be done either in class or as homework. You'll decide on the structure that feels right to you. Good workshops usually incorporate some or all of the following:

- A safe, confidential environment for people to share their life stories.
- Lots of interaction.
- A manageable number of participants: enough to get a good group dynamic going but small enough to allow equal time for all.
- A workshop leader who knows when to rein in students who talk too much.
- A workshop leader who can gently encourage all students to participate.

- Laughter! Make it fun.
- A chance for participants to socialize, get their creative juices flowing, and learn something new.

2.5 Structure

For an agenda, here's one suggestion:

- Introduction of the topic of the class (e.g. characters, setting the scene, evocative language, narrative flow)
- Excerpts that demonstrate the topic
- Discussion; sharing of ideas, stories and anecdotes; brainstorming
- Writing exercises
- Sharing (if participants choose to share)
- Feedback
- Conclusion and plans for the next meeting; any homework assignments.

Have lessons planned in advance. Never wing it. One rule of thumb is that it takes at least two hours of preparation for one hour of front-of-class time.

When the classes are finished, be sure your students know how to get in touch with you and if possible, keep their email addresses so you can contact them.

3. Coaching

Depending on your audience, you may need to tailor your coaching of memoir writers.

3.1 Coaching memoir writers

Most people need encouragement and support at some point during the life-writing process; that's why so many people join writing groups. But not everyone is a "joiner" and most would welcome one-on-one advice. That's where you, the memoir expert, come in. Coaching people who are writing their memoirs can be a positive, rewarding experience. It has the potential for regular, long-term income, because coaching is likely to be ongoing until the memoir is finished, and may well lead to editing or publishing jobs.

Depending on the client's writing skill and where they are in the process, you may be called upon to help them in any or all of these areas:

- Memory prompts and story starters
- Organization and structure
- Staying on track
- Encouragement and accountability
- Writing exercises

- Narrative flow
- Sentence structure and grammar
- A light edit and proofread

Coaching can be done in person, or by email, or via the Web. You can charge an hourly rate as you work together or offer a package deal, such as a certain number of sessions for a set price.

3.2 Coaching personal historians

As you become more experienced and known as a personal historian, you might be approached by people who want advice and information about how they too can become a personal historian. It's perfectly reasonable to charge for your time should you choose to do so.

16
ACCELERATING YOUR SUCCESS AND MANAGING BUSINESS GROWTH

Now that you've begun your business and have had some experience in all the topics we've covered so far, consider taking Quiz 2 (available on the CD-ROM) to refresh your memory and get you thinking about some important business details again.

As the months go by and your business grows, keep a clear head and a steady hand to ensure you don't burn out, veer off course, or even throw in the towel. Let me elaborate on those clichés.

1. Avoid Burnout

We've all heard the term, but what does "burnout" mean to you? To me, it means losing the balance in my life — spending too long sitting at the computer and not long enough laughing, dancing, walking, and reading. If I work too long I eventually get irritable, don't sleep well, get back pain, and otherwise lose energy and motivation. Of course, this is counter-productive to all those long hours spent at the computer. Put limits on your workday. It will motivate you to do what you need to do before quitting time. Be careful to keep balance in your life and make time for the things and people you love. If you don't, what are you working for?

2. Avoid Veering off Course

Regularly review your business plan and your marketing plan. Are you following them? You prepared them objectively based on your market research. They were also based on your vision: what you dreamed and wished for when running your own business was just a gleam in your eye. If you're not meeting your objectives, why not? What's changed? Remember that a business plan is an organic document, not set in stone. It's meant to evolve and adapt as you learn more about your customers' needs, your product, your own strengths, and what you like doing. Look hard at the areas in which you're doing well, and those areas in which you need help.

3. Definitely Don't Throw in the Towel

Even the most successful entrepreneurs have times when they ask themselves,"Why am I doing this? Why am I stressing myself out? I could go and get a job and a regular paycheck and let someone else worry about a printer that's always breaking down … "

It's on days like this when you need to take a deep breath and remember why you wanted to be your own boss. Call on your support group, whether that's your family, a friend, your mastermind group, advisory board, or professional colleagues.

If you're struggling, it might be a good investment to hire a business coach. Even with just a few sessions, she or he can help you target those areas that need improvement and show you how to gain the skills you need to succeed. There's no mysterious magic in running a successful business. It's hard work, yes, but most importantly, it's smart work. Believe in yourself, and your vision will turn into a reality.

If you like the work, the main reason you'd give up is that you're not making enough money. You feel resentful, discouraged, exhausted, and you convince yourself that "this just isn't the right business for me." You'll come up with a dozen different reasons your business is not succeeding the way you hoped: you have no proper office, you have no money for a decent computer, if only John hadn't gotten the flu, you're hopeless at talking money with potential customers.

Yes, there are bumps and lumps in life and in business. You can get over them. Persevere. If you don't have any clients at any given time, use the opportunity to educate yourself, learn something new, write a presentation, get out and network, refine your systems, or do more research into potential products you could offer. Be ready for success. And don't give up without a fight!

4. Taking Your Financial Pulse

4.1 So how are things going?

Give yourself six or nine months, but don't wait too long to begin examining your financial books. Look at your sales. Then deduct your expenses: marketing, travel, supplies, etc. Whatever's left is your net profit. Are you happy with it?

Examine which projects netted you the most profit; not the projects that had the highest price tag, but the ones that made you the most money. Focus on getting more of those types of projects.

Examine what clients and marketing strategies netted you the most profit. Look at factors like where and how you found the customers. How easy were they to find? How much effort and time did it take to get them to sign a contract? Then focus your marketing efforts on those types of clients. Here are some examples.

Marketing Effort #1: Your presentation at a high-end retirement residence was enjoyable.

You met several terrific people and your public speaking skills are improving! Timewise? Well, it took three days to prepare, and a full day travelling and giving your talk. You followed up with five residents who expressed interest in hiring you. It's now six months later and they've all said no.

Marketing Effort #2: Mother's Day was approaching, so you wrote an article for the local newspaper about a great gift for anyone's mother: her life story in a gorgeous legacy book. Your contact information was included, and you followed up with an ad for four consecutive weeks. Three people called you and one turned into a paying customer for a long family history. He gave you a glowing testimonial that you posted on your website, and two of his friends have contacted you with possible projects.

Which marketing effort paid the best dividends? Which do you think you should do more of?

Some expenses are fixed, such as overhead like electricity bills, Internet, etc. But take a good hard look at what you've spent on everything, including the "experimentals" — those things you tried. Is that networking group worth the $120 yearly membership? Did you get any customers from donating to the silent auction?

4.2 Business on a tight budget

Trim your expenses wherever you can. Here are just a few suggestions:

- Give up the $5 lattes. If you're meeting a colleague for a coffee, go to a cheaper coffee shop or invite him or her to your house. Better yet, take a walk together.

- Consolidate business trips to save gas. Meeting a client in another town? What other business can you do on the way?

- Buy used equipment rather than new.

- Check out wholesalers for office supplies or packaging.

- Paying someone to scan photos? It might be cheaper to buy a good scanner yourself (and study how to get good scans).

- Compare prices for everything you pay for, including subcontractors. Don't be afraid to negotiate.

- Borrow books from the library rather than buy them.

- Consider giving up magazine subscriptions. You can read them at the library, or view a lot of content online.

- Barter. You need some car repairs: Maybe your mechanic would like a family history. How about exchanging services? Bartering can be a great way to get "free" goods and services in exchange for your own. It might be tricky to match up the value of what each of you are providing, but when it works, it can be a great way to get what you need without handing over cash or piling up credit card debt. (Remember that the tax man wants to know about the value of the goods or services!) Canada Revenue Agency has rules about barter transactions on its website. On the home page, type "barter" in the Search field. The process is the same on the US Internal Revenue Service site.

Bottom line: pay handsomely for those things that will truly make a difference to your business, such as business coaching or a great business card. Save money wherever you can.

5. Managing Growth

5.1 Delegating, outsourcing, subcontracting

As you get more business, there will come a time when you can't possibly do everything yourself, from accounting to writing to scanning to book production — not to mention marketing so your success continues. You're going to need help. You'll want to build a team, because that's the only way to grow and increase your profits.

Now that you know what goes into a typical personal history project, think about the areas you want to do yourself and which ones you could pay someone to do. Ideally, that person will do it cheaper and better than you could do it yourself.

Finding such people is time consuming. Ask people in your network if they know anybody with the skills you need. Check professional associations and save time by looking at online portfolios. Getting a name is just the start. You have to contact the person, preferably meet face-to-face, see samples of his or her work, get references, discuss rates, and otherwise determine if this is someone you can trust and with whom you want to do business. Choose your associates very carefully. Your reputation will suffer if the work is done poorly. Not only that, you may end up paying double to get it fixed by someone else and lose a customer's goodwill.

Don't wait until you're in a panic. Stay in contact with possible subcontractors. Who knows? They might refer business to you, too.

5.2 Markup

Most business experts recommend that you bill your customer a 10–20 percent add-on to what you paid your subcontractor. Your time is worth money, too, and it's not as if you can just accept what your subcontractor sends you as final. No matter how good his or her work is, you are ultimately responsible for its quality and you'll spend a good chunk of time reviewing it. You'll also be consulting with them, preparing files and doing administrative work. Viewed this way, 20 percent sounds reasonable, doesn't it?

Yes, but you also have to take into consideration what you can reasonably charge your client. If you pay a graphic artist $70 per hour, are you ready to add $14 and charge your client $84 per hour? If not, then you have two options: find a cheaper graphic artist, or reduce your markup. That's why it's vital that you not leave things until the last moment and have to pay a premium. Try to find reliable, skilled subcontractors who don't charge more than you do, and when you do find them, hang on to them!

6. Ongoing Education, Skills Development, and Training

6.1 Running your business

Check your local government for programs for small-business owners. Some of these programs are free, and might even offer financial assistance in your start-up phase. You can get help with taxation issues, marketing, bookkeeping, legalities specific to your state or province, and more. Just as valuable is the chance to make valuable contacts. The professionals who run these workshops and seminars might well be in a position to refer you to clients.

6.2 Professional development

Never stop learning — not that that's possible. With every project, you'll improve your skills, learn more than you ever imagined about human behavior (including yours!), and vow to do something differently next time. Your best teacher is yourself, if you listen carefully.

Keep learning:

- If you're not using Word or Excel to all their capabilities, take some tutorials. It will save you time in the long run. Computer stores such as Apple offer classes or one-on-one instruction on certain programs.

- Subscribe to magazines, either online or in print, on effective marketing strategies, trends in the marketplace, negotiating, and sales.

- Search the Internet and newspapers regularly for competing or complementary new businesses in your area.

- Watch for opportunities to hear expert speakers. Networking groups often hold these types of events and you probably don't need to be a member to attend.

- You can often find free or low-cost webinars or online tutorials about marketing. They're offered by people who want you to continue taking their courses after the free session is over, but you can still pick up some good tips.

- Take advantage of e-newsletters by experts in a field. Their quick tips are often very useful and can be a swift kick in the butt to get you thinking about possible ways to get your name out there.

- Read everything you can about personal history, oral history, memoirs, memoir-writing, family history, and genealogy. Become a regular at the library. Check the magazine racks at a bookstore or convenience store for all the specialized publications about writing, genealogy, and history.

- Do a search on the Internet for the above terms and go surfing.

- Carve out a niche for yourself by becoming a specialist in an area that interests you — perhaps a skill, or a certain period in history, or a product such as art collages that tell family stories.

- Check colleges, universities, and oral history associations for courses in memoir-writing, oral history, editing, or whatever your interest is. You may find them in departments such as American Studies, Ethnic Studies, Public History, Creative Nonfiction, or Continuing Education.

- Hire an experienced personal historian to coach you, either on an as-needed basis to help you problem-solve, or for a weekly or monthly meeting by telephone, over the Internet, or in person.

- Even if you plan on outsourcing a lot of the work such as editing or graphic design, educate yourself about what these professionals do. First, you need to know what you're paying for, and second, you'll want to talk their language as you work together.

- Visit a bookbinder. If books or booklets are part of your "repertoire" you should understand the different types of bookbinding. There are lots of books you can read about the process, but there's nothing like seeing it in person at a bookbinder's shop. Most bookbinders will be happy to spend 40 minutes or so with you, particularly if there's an opportunity for future business.

- Genealogy is a close cousin of personal history and the lines of our professions often cross. Learn what genealogists do, what they read and what organizations they belong to. Consider hiring one to research your own family history — or do it yourself. Many of your clients may want to research their family tree, so find out how you can help them. Align yourself with someone you like and trust.

- Visit museums. Every city, town, and region has some sort of museum, where you'll find artefacts, documents, photographs, maps, and other items that tell the stories of days gone by.

- Take classes in your community on memoir writing.

- Get trained as a hospice volunteer.

- Keep up on the latest trends, technology, and techniques for audio capture and sound editing (if you plan on doing that).

- Stay informed about the various print-on-demand publishers' ever-increasing array of options and new technology.

- Keep up-to-date on programs offered at seniors' centers and see how your services could be used.

6.3 Connecting with kindred spirits

Being self-employed in any business can be lonely, isolated work, and as a personal historian you'll experience probably more than your fair share. Connecting with kindred spirits through various associations is invaluable. The Association of Personal Historians provides a community, ideas for new projects, new (or best) ways of doing things, business advice, marketing tips, recommendations about the latest gadgets and technology, and much more. The annual conference is three to four days of networking, educational workshops, brainstorming, expert speakers, and a chance to immerse yourself in the world of personal history with a few hundred like-minded individuals from around the world.

6.3a Oral history associations and institutions

Groups devoted to oral history have a wealth of information and educational opportunities that will help you manage a personal history project, and especially improve your interviewing skills. Baylor University's Institute for Oral History (www.baylor.edu/oralhistory) has a collection of oral histories, a "Workshop on the Web" to learn how to conduct oral history interviews and what to do with the material, and also information about how to teach oral history in the classroom. Some oral history associations have listservs with lively discussions about various issues related to oral history.

6.3b Entrepreneurial and small-business associations

Do a little digging and find a group of self-employed businesspeople. The people don't have to be in the same field; in fact, it will be refreshing to hear about other businesses. Everyone who's running a small business faces challenges, both professionally and personally.

OTHER TITLES OF INTEREST FROM SELF-COUNSEL PRESS

Low-Budget Online Marketing for Small Business

Holly Berkley

ISBN: 978-1-55180-890-1

$20.95 USD/$21.95 CAD

Large companies have huge budgets for marketing their products and services online. What's the difference between a $100,000 marketing campaign and a $1,000 campaign? Surprisingly, not much. This book teaches small-business operators how to achieve big-business marketing success on a small-business budget!

Low-Budget Online Marketing for Small Business takes you behind the scenes of successful marketing campaigns. This book will show you how to cut costs so that you can adapt the same successful marketing strategies that big companies use.

If you are looking to attract attention to your company on the Internet, this book will show you how, and with only a minimal investment! This book includes the following topics:

- Targeting your campaign
- Generating free advertising
- Email marketing
- Building Web communities
- Successful co-branding strategies
- Banner advertising
- Web design basics
- — And more!

Pricing Strategies for Small Business

Andrew Gregson

ISBN: 978-1-55180-797-3

$16.95 USD/$18.95 CAD

Pricing a product or service can make or break a small business.

It's essential to use a good pricing strategy to ensure the products or services are appealing to customers and to ensure that the company is profitable. It's not always as simple as "the lowest price wins." *Pricing Strategies for Small Business* covers the many different pricing strategies and helps readers to determine which methods are best for their small businesses.

An optimal pricing strategy will depend on more than just the business costs. Forces within a business environment such as competitors, suppliers, availability of substitute products, and customers' disposable income all come into play.

Like all books from Self-Counsel Press, this book is written in an easy-to-understand manner. It shows readers step by step how to choose the right prices for their products and services, and covers the following topics:

- Psychological pricing
- Price skimming
- Penetration pricing
- Cost plus markup
- Multiple unit pricing

Self-Counsel Press